HOW TO OWN
BITCOIN
ADVENTURE VERSION

BY JASON ARALIA

The author and publisher of this book are not wealthy, nor do they keep their tiny hodls of crypto in their homes. Why else spend all the time writing a book?! If you read and understand this book, you'll know that the small amount of Bitcoin and cryptos they might have would be very, very well protected. If one were to read the chapter on multi-sig and look for services that will hold one or more multi-sig shares securely, one might get an idea of how difficult it would be to obtain the author's investments. Just saying, don't bother.

PREFACE - HOW TO USE
THIS ADVENTURE VERSION

Owning Bitcoin is an exciting adventure that few have undertaken. If you take on this adventure, you are now a pioneer, a visionary, a market maker, a digital warrior. This adventure takes you on a journey through a tangled jungle of myth and misunderstanding, and will guide you through your Bitcoin journey. This book was designed to shape itself to the user's needs as they read through and choose the paths that interest them.

Each path requires different levels of skill to scale the mountain of knowledge.

You must find a way across the chasms of chaos by constantly considering your risk tolerance.

Every choice requires cunning to capitalize on the level of convenience that's right for you.

So, like an adventure book of old, you need to choose your own path. This book aims to teach you how to own Bitcoin—your way—by giving you the tools to discover what your method is on your journey through the world of Bitcoin.

Some parts of this book may be overwhelming or underwhelming, depending on your interests and goals. That's okay! Each chapter and subchapter has links at the bottom to help you navigate this book and read only the parts that interest you. Although the repetitiveness and link system can get annoying—if you're a read-straight-through type of person—the links are intentionally designed to help you get to the information that you want and need.

This book will advise you—repeatedly—to Do Your Own Research (DYOR). DYOR is a staple of the Bitcoin community. The crypto universe is in its infancy, changing faster than you can read this book or check a website; therefore, since this book was intentionally designed so chapters can be skipped, it repeats the DYOR mantra enough times throughout so everyone gets it. The more complicated the section of this book you are in, the more vehemently DYOR will be recommended!

There are a few parts of this book that are recommended for EVERYONE to read, no matter if you're a total noob or a Bitcoin maximalist. These chapters are listed at the end of the book in case you skipped one and want to go back. Consider a stop there once you have read the book to make sure you didn't miss anything important. You can find the list in Chapter 9 - Miscellaneous Interesting Stuff - Rated: EVERYONE.

This book may be updated for accuracy or to add new information. The book will not automatically update. If you are interested, please check for updates before each reading. Kindle will only automatically update the book for you if there is a critical revision. Updating the book may erase highlights, bookmarks, or notes that you have added to your copy.

INTRODUCTION

Do you want to know about Bitcoin, BTC, XBT, or 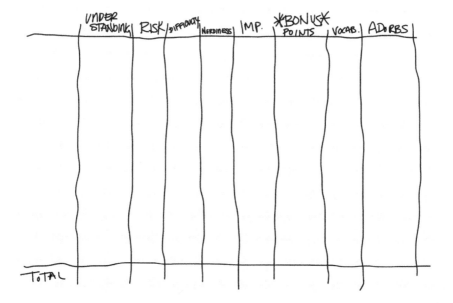? What level of difficulty would you like to start with? Once you get into Chapter 1 Subchapter Selection, click the link that seems to fit you best. If you choose to read this book cover to cover instead of using the adventure style, there will be some repetitiveness that results from creating a book formatted this way.

There is a glossary at the end of the book found at Glossary of Terminology.

Just for fun, you will find some skill points listed at the end of each chapter. These skill points are almost entirely arbitrary and have no real meaning. Print or draw this tally sheet (image below), and keep track of the points you earn here.

Every chapter you read will add to your stats as you go through. Find out what kind of adventurer you are at the end of the book! (Keep in mind this is a wholly subjective, fun exercise meant to enrich your enjoyment of the book, not make you crazy. Have fun with this!)

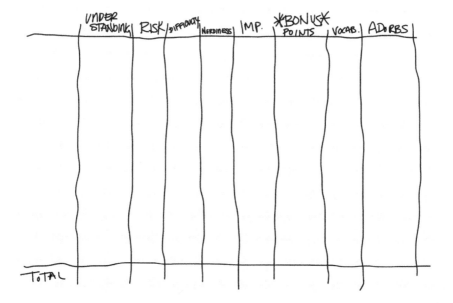

In case you can't see/read the above image, draw a horizontal line and write the categories listed below across the top of your line; each will be its own column. You'll write your points into these columns as they are awarded to you while reading the book.

Stats to draw across a horizontal line: Understanding, Risk, Difficulty, Vocabulary, Impatience, Nerdiness, Adorbs (the most difficult stat to obtain: Adorableness), Bonus Points (this category is all-encompassing, so this part will be the description).

Look, you've already earned some points just for playing along. Add them to the tally sheet that you so beautifully drew.

You earned:
+25 Understanding - For finding misspellings and realizing they are actually Bitcoin lingo.
+25 Vocabulary - Hodl: intentional misspelling of the word "hold." It's a meme.
+10 Vocabulary - Also hodling, hodled, hodler, etc.

TABLE OF CONTENTS

CHAPTER 1
SUBCHAPTER SELECTION
(Don't tally these points. They're here to help you choose which subchapter is best for you.)

Chapter 1.1 Basic
An explanation even a six-year-old could understand.
+1 Understanding

Chapter 1.2 Blockchain, Ledger, and Protocols
Great, now my six-year-old has questions.
+5 Understanding

Chapter 1.3 Origins of Bitcoin, BIP, Bitcoin Wallets
Grandpa overheard me explaining it to a six-year-old, now he has questions.
+25 Understanding

There is no basic Bitcoin explanation I can learn from! Let's skip the "what Bitcoin is" bit and learn the fundamentals! Skip to Chapter 2.1 Bitcoin's Key Features - Fundamentals
-100 Patience
+500 Understanding

CHAPTER 1.1
BASICS

People have decided that money has value. A long, long time ago, it got difficult for people to carry around big things they could use to trade for other things they needed. So instead of dragging sheep through town to trade for three chickens, people began trading money. Bitcoin is a type of money, called a cryptocurrency, that is online. Being online, it allows people to trade anywhere in the world quickly.

According to some Aristotle guy you might have heard of, good money is durable, portable, divisible, and intrinsically valuable. Bitcoin has these features. Bitcoin is also a bit like gold, except that it is digital, not physical. Many people believe that gold has value, and a growing number of people are beginning to believe that Bitcoin has value. And just like gold, it is not controlled by any government, bank, or company. Bitcoin is a global currency—a way to save your money—called a store of value.

The good thing about Bitcoin is that anyone can use it if they have access to the internet. Another good thing is that every trade anyone makes can be seen by everyone else. This means people can't cheat because everyone knows the rules.

You earned:
+10 Understanding
+250 Adorableness if you really do explain it to a six-year-old.

Continue down this path by reading further or go back to Chapter 1 Subchapter Selection

CHAPTER 1.2
BLOCKCHAIN, LEDGER, AND PROTOCOLS

Currency is a symbolic exchange of value. Instead of trading sheep for chickens, people trade currency for goods and services. Bitcoin is a usable exchange of value, so it is a currency. It is typically referred to as a cryptocurrency, even though it shares traits of both currency and money.

(Picture shows actual chain,
not actual blockchain or actual Bitcoin)

Bitcoin is based on a protocol, a list of rules and instructions that everyone agrees to follow to make the system work. For example, everyone agrees that a US dollar has the same face value as 100 US pennies.

But Bitcoin isn't quite as simple as trading cash; there is a long list of protocol rules that have to be followed to account for transactions in the system. (Luckily, the Bitcoin miners handle all the hard work. More on that later.) These protocols could technically be done on paper if you really wanted to nerd out with some crazy math, a calculator, and a few hours of spare time.

Bitcoin utilizes a digital ledger of transactions. The digital ledger—called blockchain—is the master list of all Bitcoin transactions. It has the same function as a chequebook ledger or a monthly bank statement, except that it encompasses the history of all of everyone's Bitcoin transactions, ever.

A good way to visualize the blockchain is to imagine lots of people having their own identical copy of a book that is half full. The first half of the book is a list of all the old Bitcoin transactions—a copy of the blockchain. The empty pages of the book are for writing down new trades. Imagine each page is a block, and you have to start writing on the next page once the page is filled.

What makes Bitcoin safe is that more than one person has to agree to what goes into the ledger. Once they agree, everyone copies this new transaction into their copies of the ledger. Because so many people save the old transactions, the blockchain cannot be altered; as long as it is kept by enough people to cross-check each other's ledgers for accuracy, Bitcoin's blockchain past is unchanging. To show this immutable aspect of Bitcoin, an artist chiselled some of the oldest ledger blocks into stone.

All transactions are checked against the ledger to make sure that when Bitcoin gets transferred, no one is trying to cheat. Anyone, at any time, can download the entire blockchain and verify everything that has ever happened in it. You could verify that the number of Bitcoin in circulation is accurate. You can see if anyone ever managed to duplicate or cheat. It takes some serious understanding of math to do it, but it is good to know there are people and companies out there looking at it.

The people who maintain copies of the blockchain and use it to verify transactions are called Bitcoin miners. Bitcoin miners keep an accurate copy of some or all of the ledger on their computers to help maintain the blockchain's history. When a Bitcoin transaction is created, it is sent to the network for confirmation. Once enough miners' software confirm that a transaction is complete, this transaction is added to the blockchain. If the transaction is small, it takes only 1–3 confirmations. If it's a larger transaction, 4–6 are required. Extremely large transactions will require sixty or more. Each confirmation takes approximately ten minutes.

Because of these check, recheck, and confirmation protocols, the blockchain is decentralized and irrefutable. It is generally understood—at the time of this writing—that no single person, government, organization, or evil villain controls Bitcoin (though this is an oversimplification that will be corrected throughout this book). Bitcoin's technology is global and belongs to everyone.

At the time of this writing, it seems as though Bitcoin is so widespread that it has grown beyond any central control. This makes it a digital cryptocurrency that is almost permissionless (sort of). No one needs to assign you a Bitcoin account. There is no bank that needs to check your credit score first. Even a homeless person with no identification, home address, or any worldly possessions can own Bitcoin. There are stories of homeless people who used Bitcoin ATM machines back when a Bitcoin was under $500 and invested everything they could, eventually becoming millionaires. Permissionless indeed!

A note of caution, though: many people believe that Bitcoin is unstoppable. That does not prevent anti-crypto laws or practices from rendering Bitcoin nearly worthless in the future; it just means that as long as there is a worldwide network of computers and determined enthusiasts, Bitcoin will live on.

You earned:
+50 Understanding
+30 Vocabulary

Continue down this path by reading further or go back to Chapter 1 Subchapter Selection

CHAPTER 1.3
ORIGINS OF BITCOIN

Bitcoin was the first significant blockchain-based digital currency (to solve the double-spend problem in a decentralized way). The protocols that govern it were made public on Halloween 2008 by "Satoshi Nakamoto," a pseudonym. It is not general knowledge whether Satoshi Nakamoto was an organization, government, or some forward-thinking polymath genius, but it is known that Satoshi Nakamoto had help. There is a paper trail of emails and communications that provide a fascinating rabbit hole to explore if you are so inclined.

There are typically three groups of people when it comes to beliefs about Satoshi Nakamoto.

Group one believes that Satoshi Nakamoto was a polymath genius and visionary (or a group of such people) who wanted to create a world where people could interact financially without banks and governments controlling them. The original White Paper, "Bitcoin: A Peer-to-Peer Electronic Cash System," seems to imply this sentiment. You can read it at https://bitcoin.org/bitcoin.pdf. The White

Paper is only 8–9 pages long and is a quick, easy, fascinating read that is highly recommended. The people who believe in the vision of Satoshi Nakamoto are sometimes referred to as the Bitcoin maximalists, some of which are evangelical about spreading the message and ensuring its adoption as the world's reserve currency. If Satoshi Nakamoto is/was an individual person, there is a good chance no one will ever know for sure. It seems that Satoshi wanted to remain anonymous so his system could live on, decentralized. Note: Even though the public doesn't know who he is, the masculine pronouns are used because of the masculine name he chose as a pseudonym.

Group two believes that big banks created Bitcoin to propel the idea of cryptocurrency into the media and the public mind in order to prepare us for the coming death of fiat currencies and the birth of the new CBDC (Central Bank Digital Currency). Many in this camp believe that Bitcoin will be allowed to flourish on the underbelly of the CBDC system. These people tend to believe that the big banks and governments already own most of it. Others believe that the CBDC will crush, ban, or block Bitcoin by legal, political, or technological means.

Group three doesn't care. Group three are honey badgers; honey badgers don't give a damn. Ain't nobody got time for that! Many people don't care about the origins, but do appreciate knowing the fundamentals behind why Bitcoin has become a more commonly accepted and popular investment vehicle, explained further in Chapter 2.1 Bitcoin's Key Features - Fundamentals.

Satoshi Nakamoto's Bitcoin core protocols are unchanging, but there is a layer above the core protocols where the Bitcoin community can vote to add new functionality to Bitcoin. These are called BIP (Bitcoin Improvement Proposals). More than 300 BIPs have been proposed, some of which have been voted upon and implemented. For example, BIP38—in part—is an agreed-upon encryption format. You can use any method you want to encrypt your Bitcoin wallet number so it is protected if lost or stolen; you don't need BIP38 to encrypt your Bitcoin wallet. But having a community agreed–upon method allows for more compatibility between platforms, devices, etc. More on this in Chapter 2.5 Encryption and BIP.

You earned:
+42 Understanding
+15 Vocabulary
+15 Nerdiness

Continue down this path by reading further or go back to Chapter 1 Subchapter Selection

CHAPTER 2
SUBCHAPTER SELECTION
(Don't tally these points. They're here to help you choose which subchapter is best for you.)

Chapter 2 is all about what makes Bitcoin tick. If you don't need to know the tick and are panicking to start buying Satoshis before the Bitcoin price jumps up again, skip to Chapter 3 How to Obtain Bitcoin

Chapter 2.1 Bitcoin's Key Features - Fundamentals
Seriously, this subchapter and its seven subthemes is Rated: Everyone. You should read it.
+500 Understanding

Chapter 2.2 Private Keys
This is the core part of a Bitcoin wallet. Best to read this.
+50 Core Learning

Chapter 2.3 Controlling Your Own Private Key - Self-Custody
For some, self-custody is the most important thing one can do with their Bitcoin. Others couldn't care less. Where do you fall?
+100 Self-Confidence
-100 Trust Traditional Banks

Chapter 2.4 Public Address
This is how you get paid. Everyone needs to know this.
+100 Where's My Money Going?

Chapter 2.5 Encryption and BIP
For the paranoid, careful, smart, or curious (but not all four at once).
+100 Bonus Learning

CHAPTER 2.1
BITCOIN'S KEY FEATURES
- FUNDAMENTALS

In the crypto world, "fundamentals" sometimes refer to the stats and features of a coin or token which give it value. These features are what make people willing to exchange their fiat currency for cryptocurrency. Fundamentals help determine the cryptocurrency's value.

A feature can be anything about the currency which people deem worth buying or participating in. Example fundamentals are the coin's usability as a store of value, its ability to do work, an endorsement by a celebrity, or even that it is based on a popular meme. All these fundamentals have value to someone. If it has enough value to enough people, the cryptocurrency has stronger fundamentals. If it's not valued by enough people, it has weak fundamentals. Similar to reviewing the assets owned by a company before purchasing its stock to determine the stock's worth, a cryptocurrency's value is determined by how strong its fundamentals are.

"Fundamentals" can also refer to the fundamental functions or parts of a coin or token. There is a fuzzy line between fundamental (value) and fundamental (function).

Bitcoin Fundamental #1: Transactions (Using Bitcoin Wallets)

The Bitcoin blockchain functions like a massive, global banking ledger. It keeps track of transactions. When you buy Bitcoin, you are essentially making a deposit at a massive, global bank. Your bank account is your Bitcoin wallet, and it has two parts: the private key and the public address.

An Oversimplified Analogy to Explain Transactions

Let's compare Bitcoin to a modern bank:

- Bitcoin is a bank for the entire world.
- Each Bitcoin bank account is called a Bitcoin wallet.
- The private key is like your super-secret password to your Bitcoin. Anyone who has it can get your Bitcoin. Your chequebook or ATM card would be somewhat equivalent to your Bitcoin private key. Don't share your private key.
- The public address is like your bank account number; it's the address where your Bitcoin wallet receives Bitcoin.

A Bitcoin wallet provides the same function as a bank account with an ATM card: it allows you to conduct transactions using your Bitcoin. The value of this is that you as an individual now have access to a permissionless, borderless, decentralized system to control your own transactions.

Bitcoin is not stored in a Bitcoin wallet just as your money is not stored in your cheque book. Bitcoin is stored on the blockchain just as your checking account is stored in the bank. The Bitcoin wallet is the method you use to get to your Bitcoin through signing transactions, just as a chequebook is used for writing cheques. The signing of transactions mostly happens behind the scenes, depending on what method you use to hold your Bitcoin and the services or platforms you use to manage it.

Bitcoin Fundamental #2: Permissionless

You don't need anyone's permission to pick a random Bitcoin private key address and start using it, though you may need to abide by your government's laws or your parents' rules if you are a minor (not miner, minor). Bitcoin is permissionless.

Because it is difficult to block or track—when it is implemented carefully—it has been used in nefarious activities. That being said, through the early years of Bitcoin, the US $20 note was still the number one currency used in illegal acts simply because of the US dollar's role as the world's reserve currency. Harmful acts do not make a currency bad. For example, a peaceful protest organization was cut off from funding when their government froze their bank account, so the movement switched to accepting Bitcoin donations because they could not be easily blocked. Permissionless comes with the good and the bad.

Many companies that are not so popular with credit card companies are switching to accepting only Bitcoin and other cryptocurrencies as payment. In the past, if the credit card companies refused to do business with you, you had very few options. How would you like to be told you can't start a business because some suit thinks you are too much of a risk for them? Now, a company does not need the blessings of the credit card gods to do business. Early on, this was a strong reason why people were against Bitcoin; it gave illegal and illegitimate activities a method of anonymous payment. Now, in these days of chainalytics, however, criminals are finding Bitcoin to be less and less hospitable. Even some of the oldest crimes hidden away in the blockchain data are being found and pursued by authorities.

Bitcoin Fundamental #3 Borderless

Try escaping a country by crossing a hostile border carrying a considerable amount of gold bars in your pockets; it's usually not advisable. Bitcoin private keys can be written down on a tiny piece of paper and hidden in the folded seam of your clothes. Alternatively, if you can get information out safely and securely, you could send Bitcoin or information about your Bitcoin wallet ahead of you. Bitcoin can even be stored in your mind. If you are careful, no one can discover your Bitcoin or take it away from you, and it works in any country. Imagine getting off a plane and having a currency that works everywhere universally without the need to exchange it first.

Bitcoin Fundamental #4 Decentralized

Bitcoin is decentralized (core Bitcoin where only you own and control the private key or seed phrase). No bank can freeze your Bitcoin wallet as long as your private keys are safe and secret. The original paper "Bitcoin: A Peer-to-Peer Electronic Cash System'' was a good start at its core. According to the White Paper, Bitcoin was meant to be a decentralized currency so no one could control and manipulate it. That is what makes Bitcoin unique in the crypto space. It is arguably the most decentralized coin. Even if it truly isn't, it has the lion's share of the market cap thanks to the first-mover advantage. It was designed to start small and gain momentum, unnoticed, until it dominated the space.

The fact that Bitcoin has grown so big makes it more decentralized than just about any start-up coin that might try to replace it as more decentralized. Size (market share) matters. Momentum matters. Brand awareness also matters.

Bitcoin Fundamental #5: Store of Value

There are some good arguments—for the near future—that Bitcoin may remain a store of value. Any good store of value prevents the depreciation of at least a portion of your portfolio's value. Bitcoin shows signs that it may be a very good store of value, even considering how volatile it is now. There are also arguments to support it being the best store of value created to this day. Some would say it is the ultimate store of value over the long run due to its precise 21 million Bitcoin cap. This is a hard limit written into the Bitcoin protocol. In 2020 terms, 21 million Bitcoin is only enough for each millionaire household in the United States to own about two Bitcoin.

Don't worry. To make Bitcoin more accessible to all, each Bitcoin can be broken down into 100 million Satoshis. There may come a day when people stop talking about how much Bitcoin they have and start talking in terms of Satoshis. That day might not be that far away. In 2020, one Bitcoin could have bought you a nice car, but what if you want to send your friend $20 US dollars (USD) for his birthday in Bitcoin? If you talk about the equivalent of $20 USD in Bitcoin, it would be fractional; somewhere around 0.00-something Bitcoin. But in Satoshis, $20-ish USD would be a whole number. It sounds way more impressive to give a gift of a thousand Satoshis. If Bitcoin's price continues to grow against the US dollar, there will be a point when speaking in Satoshis will make more sense. There are already talks of implementing a community agreement to switch to one of the smaller denominations listed below. Bitcoin has grown too big for its own name.

Bitcoin can also be denoted as (though some are unofficial):

- Bitcoin (BTC) = 1.0 BTC or one Bitcoin
- Bitcoin (XBT) = 1.0 BTC, same as above. This is an emerging abbreviation for Bitcoin that better conforms to the ISO (International Organization for Standardization) currency abbreviation rule where currencies without a country of origin should start with an *X*. The BTC and XBT abbreviations are interchangeable.
- Millibitcoin (mBTC) = 0.001 BTC or one-thousandth of a Bitcoin
- Microbitcoin (μBTC) = 0.000001 BTC or one-millionth of a Bitcoin
- Satoshi (sat) = 0.00000001 BTC or one-hundred-millionth of a Bitcoin

Not all of the 21 million Bitcoin are available currently. The incentive for the Bitcoin miners to support and secure the Bitcoin network is that they get paid in Bitcoin. As a huge bonus, every time a new block is completed on the blockchain, some Bitcoin is awarded to the Bitcoin miner who completed the block (oversimplification). Approximately every four years, the bonuses and fees the miners collect for completing a block are cut in half. This ensures that the supply of 21 million Bitcoin does not run out too fast.

This makes Bitcoin one of the most, if not the most, scarce but widely available assets invented so far. An analogy is gold, and as such, it is often called digital gold. Gold is a scarce resource that has a cost to mine. People have used it as a currency for thousands of years. Because people have arbitrarily decided that gold has value as a currency, it becomes a store of value and can be exchanged for fiat currency or directly for goods and services.

Bitcoin Fundamental #6: Programmable Money - Smart Contracts and DeFi

Quick primer: Smart contracts can allow the automation of business and finances. DeFi is an attempt to replace some or all of the banking industry and its financial products with partially or fully decentralized systems and platforms.

Bitcoin is digital. This seems obvious, but it gives Bitcoin a superpower; it can be used in digital systems directly. Try typing a dollar bill into your computer to pay for something. Good, now you know that doesn't work (if you tried it, I have a bridge to sell you on McCulloch Blvd N. It's seen some fire damage, but is in good condition otherwise. Accepting 42 Bitcoin, OBO).

Bitcoin is directly integrable and compatible with an ever-increasing digital world economy. For example, many cryptocurrencies—including Bitcoin—facilitate the use and implementation of smart contracts. A smart contract is like a software program that automatically executes a transaction when real-life conditions meet the terms of an agreement.

Let's say you want to create an insurance product that will pay people if their train is late. Since the trains being late or on time is a data point kept by someone or some company, and information about who has tickets for these trains is also kept as data, a smart contract with access to these pieces of information could automatically pay a customer. The company doesn't have to deal with the accounting, and customers know they will get paid automatically as long as the train and passenger information is kept up to date and accurate.

Smart contracts can be created and efficiently executed with cryptocurrencies without the need for an escrow company to hold the funds and handle the transactions. The smart contract is the escrow. As long as a smart contract is written carefully and securely, the network can handle tracking contract conditions and perform payments when these are met. Physical fiat money cannot be held directly in a digital system. This is why Bitcoin being digital allows contracts to safely hold a private key for a Bitcoin wallet and use the Bitcoin to make payments automatically without the need to involve a third-party bank or service. Every part of a smart contract can be automated and simplified, saving money, time, and hamster wheel replacements (if you are using hamsters to power your business for some reason).

Bitcoin has a part to play in the new decentralized finance space. Much of DeFi is built on smart contracts. (More on this in Chapter 5.4 DeFi.) Bitcoin has been an essential catalyst in the movement to create partially decentralized banking built mostly on smart contracts. Imagine permissionless banking; you can stake some agreed-upon equity and take out a loan without the need for a bank or government to decide if you are worth it.

Bitcoin Fundamental #7: Total Anonymity (Not)

Bitcoin is NOT anonymous. Not at all. Not even a little bit. It may be touted as one of Bitcoin's prime features, and you may be able to take steps to increase your anonymity, but every Bitcoin has a history. Chainalytics companies track and study every transaction and address by running the on-chain data through extremely sophisticated software. These companies are also connected to vast amounts of supplementary information, allowing them to see where Bitcoin is being mined, who mined it, and everywhere it goes from there. The more information they have on each Bitcoin transaction, the better picture they can paint on individual users and the crypto economy as a whole. You can take steps to obfuscate some of your on-chain and supplementary data, but every Bitcoin has a history. Check out https://studio.glassnode.com/ to see some of the macro information gathered from Bitcoin's ledger.

Despite some people believing that Bitcoin is an anonymous currency for criminals, Bitcoin is said by some to be the most precise verification of assets ever created. If a person or company wants to get a loan, they can show their Bitcoin holdings instantly. In contrast, verification of any other asset for a larger company takes massive audits. Many companies only produce these audits monthly or yearly due to the cost and difficulty.

For example, MicroStrategy is a business intelligence and cloud-based service provider that publicly announced their purchase of

38,250 Bitcoin for $425 million US dollars in mid-2020. MicroStrategy can point an investor to their Bitcoin wallets' public addresses and have those assets verified in seconds. If further verification of access to a Bitcoin wallet were required, MicroStrategy could transfer a small, previously specified amount of Bitcoin at an arranged time to prove they have access to the funds, all without exposing their private keys or incurring the cost of doing a massive audit.

There are websites where you can enter any known Bitcoin public address and see every transaction it has ever received or sent. This also provides you with the current balance and a staggering amount of additional information, if you wanted to dig deeper. This means that your uncle Bob, who sent you two hundred Satoshi for your birthday, can know everything about your Bitcoin holdings if you only deal with self-custodied wallets. One way of obfuscating your holdings and transactions is to pass them through an exchange that allows deposits and withdrawals. This won't hide much from chainalytics companies or governments which may have access to the exchanges data, but it will let you hide some of your personal data from Uncle Bob. You may not want Uncle Bob knowing exactly how many Satoshis you've been stacking (or where you spend them).

You earned:
+250 Nerdiness
+250 Understanding
+10 Bonus Points: Decentralization
+10 Bonus Points: Scarcity

Continue down this path by reading further or go back to Chapter 2 Subchapter Selection

CHAPTER 2.2
PRIVATE KEYS

The main part of a Bitcoin wallet is a very, very long number called a private key. This key gives you access to your Bitcoin, so it should never be shared with anyone who shouldn't have access to your Bitcoin. It is like the password for your bank account, except in this case, it's also the bank account. Having access to this super-secret private key lets you sign the transactions of Bitcoin you are sending out of your wallet.

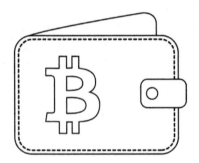

The magic of the Bitcoin wallet is that you could theoretically choose any random 256-bit number in the range defined by the Bitcoin protocol and you would have your very own Bitcoin wallet. It's between 0x1 and 0xFFFF FFFF FFFF FFFF FFFF FFFF FFFF FFFE BAAE DCE6 AF48 A03B BFD2 5E8C D036 4140 for you HEX nerds.

No one needs to assign a Bitcoin wallet to you. No bank or government knows what number you picked until you use it to make a transaction and it shows up on the blockchain. You can have as many addresses as you want! To get a new address, you can choose another number—any number—in the protocol's range. Just make sure you don't pick one that's already in use. Sorry, that was a little joke. The odds of randomly picking someone else's address are less than one in a million. Sorry, another joke. The odds are actually one in 1,461,501,637,330,902,918,203,684,832,716,283,019,655,932,542, 976. Think of it this way: if you went to the beach and marked a grain of sand as yours, dropped it during a storm, and then waited to see if anyone else ever picked up that one grain of sand, you'd be waiting a loooooooooong time.

Technically, Bitcoin wallets are just lying around with no security; they are simply loooooooong numbers. Someone could guess your private key and take all of your Bitcoin, and there would be nothing you could do about it. But the chances of someone finding your particular grain of sand on the Bitcoin beach are impossibly minuscule. Bitcoin's safety lies in the sheer number of possible private keys. Instead of having a bank issue you an account, and using technology and hackable, fallible password systems to protect your money, Bitcoin relies on the simplicity of impossibility to protect you.

This is an example of a Bitcoin wallet private key in its most basic decimal format. (Don't get snippy, number nerds. This is the Hex to Dec conversion of a Hex key.):

35240037927300304396209544059757918972878360505272642936731959666666229762248

See! It is just a number! A very long number, but a number nonetheless. That same Bitcoin wallet can also be denoted in other common notation formats (just a point of interest for the super nerds; the rest of you should skip to the next subchapter):

- Private Key WIF:
  - 5JQbhyf5Nx1kBxammQJsH7F6iiNNHWEty6piPUQpEDnMPmK5wog
- Private Key WIF Compressed (newer standard):
  - KyqABs54KspHdNL4aysrv6ZEF7bJwr4LNchbgBz7TMRB1M4Hjbv3
- Private Key Hex (64 characters of numbers 0–9 and letters A–F):
  - 4DE927964DD3239ABFD9F62916BE601F8C850CA464258FCB0C2BAEE10CF488C8
- Private Key Base64 (64 characters, newer standard)
  - Teknlk3TI5q/2fYpFr5gH4yFDKRkJY/LDCuu4Qz0iMg=

You earned:
+50 Understanding
+15 Nerdiness

Continue down this path by reading further or go back to Chapter 2 Subchapter Selection

CHAPTER 2.3
CONTROLLING YOUR OWN
PRIVATE KEY - SELF-CUSTODY

"Your keys, your Bitcoin. Not your keys, not your Bitcoin."
—Andreas Antonopoulos

You can choose to control your own Bitcoin wallet, or you can choose to allow a bank, service, or exchange to hold the Bitcoin for you. (Very thorough detail in Chapter 3 How to Obtain Bitcoin).

Warning: If you choose to hold your Bitcoin in a Bitcoin wallet you control, you must never share your Bitcoin wallet private key with anyone or anything ever, for any reason. You must not type it into an app, email, text message, etc. You must not save it on any computer or device that is connected to the internet or will ever be connected to the internet. You must not read it out loud near any listening device or nefarious person.

ANY exposure of this super-secret number is critically bad. There are bots that scan the internet, emails, text messages, and stolen information from viruses and trojan horses with only one purpose: to find and empty YOUR Bitcoin wallets! Bitcoin is decentralized; there is no one to turn to so you can get your Bitcoin back. (Though, there is a chance that some very sophisticated and expensive research could be done to trace where the Bitcoin went if the thieves are sloppy. Then, you would have to take legal action against them in the real world.) The truly paranoid among us will even cover webcams, mobile phone cameras, and all other visual recording devices when working with our private keys, just to be sure.

The private key must remain secret, especially while you learn how to use it safely. Anyone who possesses your private key has full access to your Bitcoin, and there is nothing you can do to stop them from stealing all of it, including any deposits in the future. Bitcoin wallet private keys should not be stored on the internet in any format. If you feel that anyone else may have gotten access to your Bitcoin wallet private key, consider making a new wallet, transferring all of your funds, and keeping the new one safe. ASAR (As Soon as Reasonable), remove all of the Bitcoin stored in that Bitcoin wallet and never use it again. Chapter 4.8 Cold Storage - Paper Wallet - Withdrawing Bitcoin can help with that.

Remember:

"Your keys, your Bitcoin. Not your keys, not your Bitcoin."
—Andreas Antonopoulos

You earned:
+10 Understanding
+50 Confidence

Continue down this path by reading further or go back to Chapter 2 Subchapter Selection

CHAPTER 2.4
PUBLIC ADDRESS

Public addresses are generated—through cryptography—from the private key. This public address is where Bitcoin can be sent into your wallet. Think of it like an email address for your incoming Bitcoin. Thanks to some super fancy, marvellous, spectacular math and internet magic, your public address can be calculated from your private key, but NOT the other way around. (If you want to go deeper down the rabbit hole, do a web search for "hash functions." You can spend weeks down that hole if you are a numberphile or cryptography nut).

Public addresses are 160-bit hash (more really long numbers). They can be more easily stored in a few different formats such as case-sensitive alphanumeric strings. The standard formats are currently 26–35 characters that start with either a 1, 3, or bc1.

Like an email address, this Bitcoin public address is where Bitcoin would be sent so they end up in your Bitcoin wallet. Public addresses can be shared online and with anyone safely, though take caution and be smart about it. There are some benefits to keeping your Bitcoin public address(es) out of the general public's eye. All transactions are public information on the blockchain. Anyone who knows your public address can do a web search to see every transaction that address has ever been involved in. You may not want certain people seeing just how much Bitcoin you have going in and out of your wallet, especially if you have that one friend who is always asking you for money. You may want to use multiple Bitcoin wallets, and choose different ones for different situations. People can also see every wallet an address has interacted with, so you can't just have an address that receives your Bitcoin then move it to another address to hide how much you have right now. Transferring Bitcoin onto an exchange, bank, or service may obfuscate where your Bitcoin goes.

Private keys can produce many different versions of public addresses. Even though these representations don't look like numbers, they represent the same underlying number:

- Public Address:
    - 18mVna4WByf3cAdGRmYmM3kNYPnvUQbvTz
- Public Address Compressed (newer standard):
    - 12LMgBAHJDvwK6p6iBsBeFzVK2VStU97pk
- Hex Key (130 characters of numbers 0–9 and letters A–F):
    - 0441776935EECAB2D45858BE1AAC2FFF1C59B1A825 3FE593E32E8516F8BC3D3AF36608C1653531384AB3 B11DBB43F3465F034085ACA6612255934A01959EA 5E655
- Hex Key Compressed (130 characters of numbers 0–9 and letters A–F, newer standard):
    - 0341776935EECAB2D45858BE1AAC2FFF1C59B1A825 3FE593E32E8516F8BC3D3AF3

These keys can be represented as QR codes to make using them easier and more accurate. Typing in these long numbers is prone to human error. So typically, you want to copy/paste or scan the QR codes of these numbers, since any Bitcoin sent to the wrong address is gone forever.

This QR code is the same as the Public Address Compressed above, but in a more scannable format which most QR apps on smartphones can read. This book accepts donations to this address if you need to practise sending Bitcoin somewhere. :<)

You earned:
+100 Understanding
+142 Nerdiness
+100 Nerdiness Bonus if you understood the different key formats.

Continue down this path by reading further or go back to Chapter 2 Subchapter Selection

CHAPTER 2.5
ENCRYPTION AND BIP

Cryptocurrencies use cryptography as part of their encryption.

BIP is a system of improving Bitcoin.

Alright, that's this chapter done! Let's go to Chapter 3 How to Obtain Bitcoin.

Oh. You're still here? OK, here is a bit more, then:

Bitcoin's use of cryptography is just one layer of encryption that allows you to accept Bitcoin at your public address without exposing your private key to the world. This encryption is core to Bitcoin. But wait...there's more! Bitcoin can be improved over time by the community. Bitcoin has another layer of encryption based on community agreed–upon standards. These community upgrades to Bitcoin are done through the BIP system—Bitcoin Improvement Protocols. There have been way more than fifty BIPs proposed. Some are implemented, many are not. This book will only cover two of them, BIP38 and BIP39, but a list can be found and enjoyed (if you are into that kind of thing) at https://github.com/bitcoin/bips. Just remember that these BIP are not built into the Bitcoin protocols, they rest on top. Typically, they are instructions about how the market interacts with Bitcoin's core protocols.

BIP38 is a protocol add-on to Bitcoin that lets you encrypt your private key with a password to make it more secure in case it is lost or stolen. If someone has your normal (non-BIP38 encrypted) Bitcoin wallet private key, then they have complete access to your Bitcoin. But, if someone has access to your BIP38 encrypted private key, it is useless without the password you used to encrypt it. Because BIP38 is a standard agreed upon by the Bitcoin community, if you know your encrypted private key and the password, you can use any BIP38-compliant tool to get to your Bitcoin.

BIP39 is an encryption protocol that lets you use seed words or a seed phrase—an agreed-upon list of words—which can be used to gain access to your Bitcoin. Seed words are typically used as a recovery method when using hardware wallets and software wallets. Since the list of words is agreed upon by the community, you can use your seed words on any BIP39-compliant platform or device, and you'll know that your seed phrase will work. And for the extremely paranoid or those in danger, seed words allow a person to store their Bitcoin in their MIND much easier than random-seeming alphanumeric private keys! That's right! As long as a person can remember—and keep secret—the twelve or twenty-four seed words memorized in order, they can cross borders or flee governments while bringing their Bitcoin with them stored only in their own brain! (There are other methods for brain wallets better suited for short-term emergencies explained in Chapter 4.6 Cold Storage - Paper Wallet - Digital Version. Look midway down the chapter for "Brain Wallets" as a bullet point.) Many professional hardware wallets Chapter 4.2 Cold Storage - Hardware Wallet - Professional and software solutions Chapter 4.5 Cold Storage - Software Wallet have compatibility with BIP38 so you can be assured of recovery even if the method you used to encrypt it is unavailable.

An interesting note: Because no two words in the BIP39 seed phrase list share the same first four letters, you only need the first four letters of each seed word to use your seed phrase to recover your Bitcoin. For three-letter words, include a blank as the fourth character. Saving only the first four letters can simplify writing down or engraving your seed phrase for archival purposes.

You earned:

+20 Vocabulary

+25 Nerdiness if you went to the GitHub address to research BIPs

Continue down this path by reading further or go back to Chapter 2 Subchapter Selection

CHAPTER 3
HOW TO OBTAIN BITCOIN

Obtaining Bitcoin comes down to three basic methods: someone can get it and let you borrow theirs, you can get it and custody it yourself, or you can get exposure to it through owning shares of financial products that own Bitcoin.

The three most important things to keep in mind when choosing a Bitcoin holding strategy are ease of use, risk tolerance, and ownership (who has custody and where is it). As you move through this chapter, you can choose the method that interests you the most, but keep these three points in mind. If you aren't sure how you want to hold your Bitcoin, read this chapter from top to bottom until you find where you feel most comfortable. You can also diversify your holdings between strategies, and for some, this might be advisable. This book will provide you with the basics. Do your own research!

Risk and Digital Banking

Please keep in mind that in a digital world, no system of holding ANY currency—including Bitcoin—is completely foolproof or guaranteed. Just like with a traditional bank, anything from hacks, theft, mismanagement, mistakes, errors, misplacement of keys, and a host of other problems could make your Bitcoin wallet unusable or unexpectedly empty. There are plenty of risks when participating in a digital world.

Many people believe that the fiat money they deposit in a traditional bank belongs to them. The banks feel otherwise. Technically, you don't own the money you deposit in a traditional bank. The bank is borrowing the money from you, and they provide you with a benefit in return. It is the same with Bitcoin. Your balance on exchanges, banks, or services may say you have three Bitcoin, but you don't; you have a balance. If you don't solely know and control the private key to your Bitcoin, you don't own actual Bitcoin; you have a balance. This comes with benefits and risks.

There is NO absolute, 100 percent safe and guaranteed way to store Bitcoin for yourself, nor is there an absolute, 100 percent safe and guaranteed way for someone else to do it for you. You have to choose the strategy that feels the most comfortable for you based on your risk tolerance, your intention of how you'll use your Bitcoin, and your tech savvy.

It is certainly not always best to self-custody your Bitcoin. But, if you don't own your keys and keep them secret, you don't own Bitcoin. If something were to happen to the exchange, bank, or service, you'd be out of luck because Bitcoin is decentralized; there is no authority you can go to that can help you if your Bitcoin is lost or stolen. Research the methods that feel the most comfortable for your risk tolerance, and consider diversifying by using multiple holding methods.

Potential risks are reviewed in detail in Chapter 6 Risk and Everything Else and in Chapter 6.9 Excess Paranoia.

If you are storing life-altering amounts of Bitcoin, you should probably get professional help. There are industrial services out there for very valuable accounts.

You earned:
+10 Risk
+50 Confidence

CHAPTER 3
SUBCHAPTER SELECTION

(Don't tally these points. They're here to help you choose which subchapter is best for you.)

Chapter 3.1 Banks and Services

I wanna keep this as simple as possible. Show me the easiest way to buy Bitcoin.

+100 Simplicity

-10 Trust

-100 Self-Custody

Chapter 3.2 Exchanges

I want more options. I want more altcoins. I want to trade.

+80 Simplicity

-10 Trust

-100 Self-Custody

+100 Trading

Chapter 3.3 ETFs
(Recommended reading for all)

Wait. Exchange-traded funds can do what now?!

+500 Simplicity

-100% Taxes?

-100 Self-Custody

Chapter 3.4 Mining Your Own Bitcoin

For the fanatics, numberphiles, and nerds, but not for quick profits.

+5 Simplicity

+1000 Self-Custody

+100 Hodl

Chapter 3.5 OTC, Buying Others' Bitcoin
For the rogues and sneaky ones.
+20 Simplicity
+1000 Sneak
+100 Hodl

Chapter 3.6 Dollar-Cost Averaging
(Recommended reading for all)
Don't try and time the market:
+1000 Simplicity
+100 Intelligence
+100 Automation
+100 Self-Custody
+100 Hodl

Look, I already know how to buy Bitcoin. I'm just here to learn about how to custody my very own Bitcoin! Get me there quickly before the exchanges freeze withdrawals. Skip to Chapter 4 I Can Be My Own Bank
-100 Simplicity
+100 Trust
+1000 Self-Custody
+250 Impatience* (Add to your tally sheet if you click the link above!)

CHAPTER 3.1
BANKS AND SERVICES

Banks and services buy and sell Bitcoin using their own Bitcoin wallets. They own the Bitcoin, then they let you pretend you own the Bitcoin, when in reality, you just have a balance. Banks and services (and exchanges in the next subchapter) are considered Layer 2. This means that they are not a part of the Bitcoin core protocol. Layer 2 might sound bad at face value, but Layer 2 is the only thing that will save Bitcoin as it becomes more widely adopted! See Chapter 6.8 Bitcoin Decentralized Fallacy - Layer 1, FIGHT! Banks and services are by far the easiest and potentially second-safest places to buy and store Bitcoin. Examples of services are PayPal and Robinhood. (There are many others, and more are popping up every day.)

Some banks or services don't accept customers from certain geographic locations. If you understand the implications and are OK with the risks, you can use a VPN like https://nordvpn.com/ to access these sites. If you don't understand VPNs, stick with the companies that are in regions that want your business.

Checklist for choosing a bank or service:

- What country do you want your Bitcoin to reside in? For example, the same country as where you live?
- Look for fees. Sometimes fees are dependent on what method you use for funding your account. For example, some banks or services charge higher fees if you use a debit card vs a money transfer.
- What coins and tokens are available on that bank or service? Do they have DOGE, if that is a coin you want to trade in?

Pros:
- Simplicity and speed.
- Banks and services will feel the most familiar compared to stocks or traditional banking.
- No messing about with Bitcoin wallets or keys.

- You don't even need a basic understanding of Bitcoin.
- You can move your money in and out of these places easily and quickly.
- If the bank or service is adequately secured and insured, it is potentially the safest place to keep your money in Bitcoin, but there are still risks.
- Layer 2 increases the speed, scope, function, etc., of Bitcoin by reducing the need to rely on Bitcoin's slow global transaction speed.
- Layer 2 makes Bitcoin accessible to all who have access to these widely available banks and services.
- Layer 2 tracks your transactions more like a traditional bank: since you don't actually own any underlying Bitcoin, your transactions do not show on-chain.
- Passing the Bitcoin you self-custody through a service or exchange can help obfuscate your Bitcoin holdings from public view. It won't do much to hide your holdings from the chainalytics companies and governments, though.

Cons:

- This is not for you if you want the responsibility of keeping custody of your own Bitcoin.
- "Your keys, your Bitcoin. Not your keys, not your Bitcoin." — Andreas Antonopoulos
- You don't technically own any Bitcoin. The bank or service owns the Bitcoin, and they pretend that you own some of it, which is fine, but fundamentally, it is NOT the same as owning Bitcoin. You own a balance.
- Some of these banks and services won't allow you to withdraw your Bitcoin to a private key.
- There is no guarantee that the bank or service won't lose your/their Bitcoin. Even if they have insurance, in the event of an extensive hack, the insurance company may not be solvent enough to get your Bitcoin back. Insurance can only do so much.
- There is no guarantee that the country the bank or service resides in won't seize or freeze your account.

- Layer 2 is where Bitcoin loses most of its anonymity. Buying Bitcoin through a bank or service increases the amount of information the chainalytics companies have on your use of Bitcoin.
- Depending on the bank or service's country of residence, they may require KYC (Know Your Customer), where you have to upload personal information, like photos of your IDs, to prove who you are.
- Depositing actual Bitcoin does not guarantee the right to withdraw actual Bitcoin in the future.

You earned:
+50 Understanding
+25 Confidence

Continue down this path by reading further or go back to Chapter 3 Subchapter Selection

CHAPTER 3.2
EXCHANGES

If you plan to trade your Bitcoin like a stock or want more options for buying altcoins, an exchange will be much like the banks and services in Chapter 3.1 Banks and Services, but with some key differences and benefits. This book won't be covering the topic of trading Bitcoin, but it is suggested that you only trade with Bitcoin that you are financially able to lose. More in Chapter 6.4 Don't Bet the Farm. Trading is gambling, and you are gambling against some of the smartest traders, bots, and artificial intelligence in the world. Examples of exchanges are Kraken, SwissBorg, Binance, Phemex, and Gemini.

Some exchanges don't accept customers from certain geographic locations. If you understand the implications and are OK with the risks, you can use a VPN like https://nordvpn.com/ to access these sites. If you don't understand VPNs, stick with the companies that are in regions that want your business.

Checklist for choosing an exchange:

- What country do you want your Bitcoin to reside in? For example, the same country as where you live?
- Look for fees. Sometimes fees are dependent on what method you use for funding your account. For example, some exchanges charge higher fees if you use a debit card vs a money transfer.
- What coins and tokens are available on that exchange? Do they have DOGE, if that is a coin you want to trade in?
- What features do you need? Examples: margin/leveraged trading, trailing stop losses, spot trading, futures trading, options trading.

These pros and cons are in addition to the ones from Chapter 3.1 Banks and Services.

Pros:

- The ability to engage in Bitcoin and cryptocurrency trading.
- Most exchanges will allow you to withdraw real Bitcoin to a personally held Bitcoin wallet or onto another exchange.
- Most exchanges have more altcoin choices than most banks and services if you want to get more adventurous.
- If you choose an exchange which allows whitelisting, it can greatly increase security. This allows you to add crypto wallet addresses that you control or trust, and limit withdrawals to these addresses only. When you (or an attacker) attempt to add other addresses, it typically takes 48 hours, and will usually email or text you a warning. If your exchange account gets hacked but your wallets are safe, it reduces the risk of successful theft.

Cons:

- Trading is gambling! There are studies which show that most people do worse with their own trading of stocks than if they had done dollar-cost averaging or just bought and forgot.
- You take on a lot of risk when you trade (gamble).

You might consider dollar-cost averaging as an alternative to trading. More about dollar-cost averaging (DCA) in Chapter 3.6 Dollar-Cost Averaging

Continue down this path by reading further or go back to Chapter 3 Subchapter Selection
+25 Impatience
+5 Difficulty

CHAPTER 3.3
ETFS

An ETF—exchange-traded fund—is a type of investment fund. ETFs are one of the ways to experience the gains (and losses) of Bitcoin inside a retirement fund. For example, the author has a friend across the pond that knows a person who knows a person that bought some Bitcoin-based ETFs inside their Roth IRA. They mentioned something about Roth IRAs potentially providing a place for their investment in Bitcoin's value to grow (or shrink) tax-free or some-thing like that. They also mentioned they consulted with a tax specialist and a financial advisor, or something.

Pros:
- ETFs don't require you to understand Bitcoin and how to in-vest in it. ETFs let someone else worry about such complicated things. You buy it, they manage it.
- Ask your tax professional! If you ask them in the year 2020, tell them to stop being a killjoy when they tell you that Bitcoin is a Ponzi scheme, and to research the tax code for you. If you ask them in the year 2021, they will recommend their favourite Bitcoin ETFs or mixed crypto ETFs.
- Ask your tax specialist about the tax implications of making gains when owning ETFs within various funds like IRAs and Roth IRAs.

Cons:
- "Your keys, your Bitcoin. Not your keys, not your Bitcoin." — Andreas Antonopoulos
- You definitely don't actually own any single Bitcoin through an ETF.
- Ask your financial advisor! ETFs are highly regulated and come with a whole set of complications and risks that won't be covered here.

- You must trust the ETF-issuing company and leadership to do a good job for you.
- You buy it, they manage it, and then they charge for it. Some ETFs charge recurring maintenance fees, and they can be very expensive. Keep an eye out for these, so they don't surprise you in the end.

Reminder: This book is for entertainment and education. It is not financial advice. You can correctly assume that the author is a plebeian with absolutely no idea what they are writing about, so do your own research, especially when it comes to investment funds and the tax implications of such things.

You earned:
+25 Impatience
+10 Difficulty
Continue down this path by reading further or go back to Chapter 3 Subchapter Selection

CHAPTER 3.4
MINING YOUR OWN BITCOIN

Bitcoin mining deserves its own book, and there are plenty of thorough books out there. These are the key points you might be interested in to understand your investment in Bitcoin better. Most people should skip to Chapter 4 I Can Be My Own Bank, especially if you have no interest in mining. The TL;DR is that mining is highly competitive, so profits are tight, and that mining is the backbone of Bitcoin. Competitive mining is actually the core of what keeps Bitcoin secure. Since miners are the backbone of the system, some believe they partly or directly control Bitcoin's value by hodling or selling the Bitcoin they earn at the prices they see fit to take profits or to pay for their cost of mining. Nerds, read on!

The massive number of computers that store, verify, calculate, and update the blockchain are the backbone of Bitcoin's system and are called miners or mining rigs. Every on-chain transaction must be verified and added to the blockchain before it is official. This is why on-chain Bitcoin transactions have fees, also called gas fees. Miners convert electricity and computing power into hash power—a fancy word for calculations and math magic. In oversimplified terms, participating in the Bitcoin hashing process earns a miner part of the gas fee paid for the transactions they assist with. For more details, do a web search for "Bitcoin mining pools."

There is another incentive for mining; there is a near 0 percent chance that a mining computer might complete the current block and earn a significant bonus of Bitcoin. To understand Bitcoin's sheer size, you should know that over a million mining computers were estimated to be running in 2020. Are you thinking about becoming a Bitcoin miner? Know your competition and goals first. There are companies out there with over 200,000 machines. These are not powerful personal computers; these are highly specialized rigs for extreme hash rates that blow away even gaming computers for speed and per-Bitcoin expense. If you want to buy one for your home, search for "Bitcoin miner" in the shopping section of your favourite search engine.

Some companies run Bitcoin mining farms in frigid climates, powered by extremely cheap (or free), excess, green electricity. You probably can't compete with this, but don't let that stop you from learning how to mine or trying to do it yourself, if it interests you. If you leave your personal computer on all day, and the processor or video card runs idle, why not make a little extra Bitcoin on the side? If the price increases enough after that, it might even pay for the additional electricity it uses.

Bitcoin Halving: Approximately every four years, the Bitcoin earned from mining blocks is cut in half. This is called halving, and is probably a significant part of the Bitcoin market value. A Bitcoin block is mined approximately every ten minutes. Every 210,000 blocks mined causes a so-called halving. This timing is built into the Bitcoin core protocol. As an incentive to early Bitcoin miners, massive amounts of Bitcoin (in today's standards) were awarded to miners for completing a block on the blockchain. But every 4-ish years, the award is cut in half. So what happens if there are too many miners mining? If more miners join in, Bitcoin's protocol adjusts the difficulty automatically so that block completion remains at around ten minutes. Don't ask how it's done; it's magic.

The nice thing about this consistency is that it makes predicting some of the aspects of Bitcoin much easier. For example, some have calculated that the last Bitcoin will be mined somewhere around 2140 if the protocol stays mostly unchanged. Bitcoin will have probably grown, changed, morphed, or even died by then, though. The next time someone tells you that Bitcoin will die when mining becomes too expensive, remember that some miners will give up if the expense of mining gets too high. This all happens organically; commercial mining companies will shut off some or all of their mining equipment when their costs of production become too high. You can see network difficulty by going to http://Blockchain.com or https://studio.glassnode.com/ and looking for "Network Difficulty" to see where Bitcoin is now.

One other reason to do mining is to ensure that transactions can be completed. Companies which plan to accept payments in Bitcoin can run a mining machine of their own that keeps an up-to-date copy of the blockchain for reference when receiving payments. Since transactions can take anywhere from a few minutes to a few hours to pass through the Bitcoin system for final on-chain verification, there is a serious benefit to verifying available funds when accepting Bitcoin as a payment.

If you want to learn more about running the Bitcoin core mining software, go to https://Bitcoin.org and read the information they provide. The download for a full node is enormous and can take hours, days, or even weeks, depending on your internet speed. You also need a lot of storage space on the computer, space which you could otherwise be filling with Steam games.

Instead of directly mining Bitcoin, you can sell your hashing power to a company that manages the system for you. Many pay directly in Bitcoin. If you're going to sell your hashing power, there are many companies you can work with. Do a web search for "sell hash power" then research these companies to pick one that works for you.

You earned:
+10 Understanding
+10 Vocabulary

Continue down this path by reading further or go back to Chapter 3 Subchapter Selection

CHAPTER 3.5
OTC, BUYING OTHERS' BITCOIN

Buying Bitcoin directly from a person/entity/company—from one Bitcoin wallet directly to another Bitcoin wallet—is called OTC or Over-the-Counter.

One of the last bastions of limited anonymity remaining when getting hold of Bitcoin is the ability to buy Bitcoin directly from a miner. That Bitcoin could, in theory, have only four pieces of information attached to it: which miner mined it, when, what amount they transferred to you, and when that transfer happened. Potentially, you could obfuscate how much you paid for the Bitcoin and who you are, assuming the Bitcoin miner doesn't make this information available.

There may come a day when OTC is one of the only ways remaining to buy actual Bitcoin and put them into self-custody. If a real Bitcoin shortage happens, exchanges, banks, and services may stop allowing withdrawals of their Bitcoin liquidity.

Also, buying Bitcoin from any person who has it in cold storage could work, but slightly more information would then be available to the chainalytics companies, especially if the person is someone you know personally.

To make OTC work for anonymity's sake, you would need to find a way to pay them that does not use KYC (Know Your Customer). If you pay them with a credit card or other means where your personal information is attached, it defeats OTC's anonymity. If you are not trying to conceal your purchase, then don't worry about how you do it. OTC is not only for obfuscation.

You earned:
+10 Vocabulary
+10 Confidence

Continue down this path by reading further or go back to Chapter 3 Subchapter Selection

CHAPTER 3.6
DOLLAR-COST AVERAGING (DCA)

This section couldn't find a perfect home anywhere else in the book, so it squashed itself in here. Many banks, exchanges, and services offer DCA within their platforms, or you can use a service whose only business is providing DCA. This book is not financial advice; this chapter is here as an acknowledgement of another method to buy Bitcoin.

Dollar-Cost Averaging is a method of buying an asset at a set interval. For example, you could have a service automatically buy Bitcoin for you once a month/week/day/whatever. The point of this—people say—is that you can't time the market. If you try to buy low and sell high without a crystal ball to tell the future, you might do worse than just buying it regularly. For example: If you DCA buy regularly in a market where the price is going up, you will make a profit! You will make less of a profit than you would have if you had just bought a lump sum, but it will still be a profit! On the other hand, if you are buying in a market that is losing value (maybe you thought it would pick back up soon, or just don't care as long as you are adding to your stack of Bitcoin, especially when you are buying now at a discount), you lose less through DCA than you would have if you had bought a lump sum before the price fell.

The last and most important reason for DCA is consistency and regularity. Letting a service automatically buy Bitcoin for you at an interval means that you know you'll be putting at least some of your hard-earned money into an asset you believe has value. Maybe you don't have the amount of money you wish you could spend on it right now, but if you DCA in, you'll have more Bitcoin than not buying at all.

Services like https://www.swanbitcoin.com/HowToWonBitcoin can assist with DCA. Swan Bitcoin will send your Bitcoin—bought at an automatic interval—to the Bitcoin wallet of your choosing. Chapter 4 I Can Be My Own Bank has many methods for creating Bitcoin wallets you could use for this. One of the reasons Swan Bitcoin's fees are low is that they don't custody your Bitcoin. They charge you, then let a third-party company purchase the Bitcoin and transfer it directly to your Bitcoin wallet.

You earned:
+15 Impatience
+15 Bonus Points: Auto-Debit FTW

Continue down this path by reading further or go back to Chapter 3 Subchapter Selection

CHAPTER 4
I CAN BE MY OWN BANK
- SELF-CUSTODY

If you store your Bitcoin within a fully offline method, like writing it down or using a hardware wallet, you are keeping your Bitcoin in what is called cold storage.

One of the core beliefs that seem to be portrayed in the Bitcoin White Paper is the universal human right to the self-custody of wealth and finances. Bitcoin and cryptocurrencies provide you with an avenue to be your own bank and ensure you have control over your money. This prevents governments from directly taking your money. It prevents banks and organizations from stopping you from having a bank account or spending your money due to discrimination. The emerging crypto space gives all people financial freedom, even people that don't have access to the internet but have access to Bitcoin ATMs, for example.

Here, you will learn about some methods for Bitcoin self-custody with little to no third-party involvement. In some ways, self-custody can be more complicated and riskier, but some people feel strongly that Bitcoin self-custody is an absolute necessity.

When you buy Bitcoin in certain places—like exchanges—you can withdraw the Bitcoin and send it to the address of your choice. You can also receive Bitcoin directly from other people to your own address. Self-custody transactions will be on-chain, so they won't be anonymous. See Chapter 2.4 Fundamentals - Fundamental #7: Total Anonymity (Not). You don't ever own actual Bitcoin until you transfer it into your own Bitcoin wallet, where you—and only you—know the private key or seed phrase. You effectively become your own bank and get to enjoy all of the risks and responsibilities that come with the benefits.

If you use an offline electronic device to store and manage your self-custody Bitcoin, it is called a hardware wallet. If you use any non-electronic method to store Bitcoin, it is usually referred to as a paper wallet, even if no paper is involved.

None of this is financial advice. You need to do your own research. If you follow the instructions improperly or something has changed in the Bitcoin protocols in the time since the publishing of this book, you could lose everything. If you use any of these methods, it is strongly recommended to test them with small amounts of Bitcoin before using them for larger amounts. Some of these methods are easier, such as hardware wallets, while others are for tinkerers and the experienced Bitcoiners. This book hopes to help you decide which methods are best for you. Remember, you can diversify your holdings between methods for simplicity, safety, and greater anonymity.

You earned:
+25 Difficulty

CHAPTER 4
SUBCHAPTER SELECTION
(Don't tally these points. They're here to help you
choose which subchapter is best for you.)

Chapter 4.1 Cold Storage - Smartphone with TEE Chip Hardware Wallet (Rated Everyone)
(Recommended reading for all)
This technology is going to be the new normal soon. I better learn it!
+100 Simplicity
+100 Convenience
+100 Portability
-100 Hodl

Chapter 4.2 Cold Storage - Professional Hardware Wallet
I don't trust anyone! But I also want the easy way to custody my own Bitcoin.
+80 Simplicity
+80 Portability
+100 Hodl

Chapter 4.3 Cold Storage - Home Brew Hardware Wallet
I love to tinker and have old electronics lying around on most counters.
-10 Simplicity
+60 Portability
+99 Hodl
+101 Tinkering

Chapter 4.4 Cold Storage - Unsafe but Convenient Hardware Wallet
If you are what you eat, then I'm cheap, fast, and easy.
-1000 Safety
+100 Convenience
+60 Portability
-100 Hodl

Chapter 4.5 Cold Storage - Software Wallet
I like to tinker with software more than hardware (may require two computers).
+50 Simplicity
+50 Hodl
-100 Portability
+100 Utility

Chapter 4.6 Cold Storage - Paper Wallet Generators
Make a Bitcoin wallet on almost any device with a browser! (Offline is best.)
+100% Cost Savings
+50 Simplicity
+100 Hodl
+100 Tinkering

Chapter 4.7 Cold Storage - Physically Archiving Keys and Seeds
I'd like what I did in the last subchapter to be somewhat flood and fireproof!
+50 Simplicity
+100 Hodl
+100 Tinkering
+50 Durability

Chapter 4.8 Cold Storage - Paper Wallet - Withdrawing Bitcoin
I made a paper wallet, but how do I get to my Bitcoin?
+100 Convenience
-100 Hodl

Chapter 4.9 Multi-Signature
(Recommended reading for all)
OK, I've got it. Bitcoin is kinda like an ATM card. But how can I protect my Bitcoin wallet?
-100 Simplicity
+1000 Encryption
+1000 Security
+1000 Redundancy
+1000 Access Management

Chapter 4.10 Staking

I love interest almost as much as I love stake. How do I get interest on my Bitcoin?

+100% Interest

-100 Hodl

+50 Risk

Look, enough with how to store Bitcoin. I'll come back to that! Right now, I'm curious about what altcoins are. They sound fun! Skip to Chapter 5 Altcoins Intro

-10 Patience

CHAPTER 4.1
COLD STORAGE – SMARTPHONE WITH TEE CHIP HARDWARE WALLET (RATED EVERYONE)

Smartphones with a specialized secure cryptocurrency chip are coming to the market. This chip—in theory—should enable you to carry reasonable amounts of Bitcoin and cryptocurrencies with you in your phone's dedicated storage. With some magic, fairy dust, and something called Trusted Execution Environment (TEE), the mobile phone can safely store access to your cryptos in a special isolated memory. Your phone's core operating system cannot directly access this memory, even if your phone is compromised by viruses or hacking.

Note: your Bitcoin is not stored in your phone; access to your Bitcoin is stored there. Regardless of how you own Bitcoin, it's always stored on the blockchain. As long as your phone is secure, the technology is implemented properly, and you have your recovery information stored safely, losing or breaking your phone will not affect the Bitcoin stash stored there (in most cases).

Because this is an emerging technology, you'll need to be careful when using it. It is not recommended to put all of your savings and retirement into a Bitcoin wallet stored on your phone. Maybe just put in some pocket money until you are absolutely sure you know what you are doing. Once you know what you are doing, you may even conclude that putting all of your savings and retirement on your phone is still a bad idea! If you ever feel comfortable with this much risk, research the Dunning-Kruger Effect. Realize you are at the first peak on the graph. If this is still you, don't google what the first peak on the Dunning-Kruger Effect graph is called, and just trust this book. Keeping large amounts of digital currencies on your mobile phone is a bad idea in almost every single scenario.

Through the use of elves, fairies, or something equally awesome, the phone can send payment requests by glittering magic dust through API calls to the Trusted Execution Environment. API calls are the method through which two separate software systems can talk to each other to ask questions and return answers while remaining otherwise isolated. API calls are the social distancing of the programmer world. These payment requests can be securely signed within this TEE chip, allowing your private keys to function while isolated from viruses and other malware on the phone or connected devices. There is still a risk of fraudulent payment requests being sent through these API calls if the phone is compromised, but your private keys shouldn't be exposed.

There is also a risk—though very unlikely—that someone gaining access to your phone, taking it apart, and reading the chip directly could get access to your private keys. If your phone is lost, stolen, or compromised, it may be best to transfer all funds to a new secure wallet as soon as reasonable. There is always a possibility that a bug or exploit could be found in the software or hardware design which exposes you to risk; as previously mentioned, this is an emerging technology. These are only a small sampling of the reasons you should NOT put significant amounts of crypto in a smartphone or other device you plan to carry around with you.

It's recommended to use at least some—if not all—of the security features available for these Bitcoin wallets. Also, make sure you use the recommended recovery seed phrases or backup keys. Store these backup keys or phrases in a safe, secure place. You don't want a lost or broken phone to be the single point of failure which makes you lose your Bitcoin and other cryptocurrencies! Bitcoin is decentralized; there is no tech support, no help desk. Bitcoin doesn't have a home office, or someone who can just fix it for you.

You earned:
+10 Understanding
+50 Risk

Continue down this path by reading further or go back to Chapter 4 Subchapter Selection

CHAPTER 4.2
COLD STORAGE - PROFESSIONAL HARDWARE WALLET

A specialized hardware wallet is an electronic device which allows you to manage your Bitcoin wallet and assists with transactions. These devices store your private key and attempt to keep it safe while also simplifying the use of a Bitcoin wallet.

A hardware wallet has two hardware components inside and a software component to bridge the parts. Inside the device is a chip mostly isolated from the world which contains your private key. The second chip allows the user interface to create transactions that the first chip signs for. Together, these two internal components can create and sign transactions to spend Bitcoin from your private key to a public address (like your friend's Bitcoin wallet for their birthday!). Then, the software component submits the signed transactions to the Bitcoin network, where they will eventually get recorded to the blockchain if all goes as planned.

These devices handle the incredibly complicated process of creating, signing, and transmitting these transactions to the Bitcoin network for verification and inclusion on-chain. These devices work much like the TEE chips described in Chapter 4.1 Cold Storage - Hardware Wallet - Smartphone with TEE chip. Some hardware wallets use a computer or mobile phone to create the transactions. More advanced hardware wallets can do every step unassisted.

Many of these hardware devices will provide you with a recovery seed phrase. This allows a hardware wallet to regenerate identical private keys on a replacement device. A BIP39-compliant device will create a twelve or twenty-four word seed phrase. Trying to write down, store, or remember 12–24 words in order is much easier than the full, seemingly random, case-sensitive, alphanumeric Bitcoin wallet private key. Remember, Bitcoin is stored on the blockchain.

Your seed phrase is your only backup to restore access to your Bitcoin.

TL;DR: If you know your seed phrase, you can enter it into any BIP39-compliant device or compliant online service, and instantly have access to your Bitcoin wallet in cases where your device is lost, stolen, or otherwise irreparably damaged. This means, if your chosen device or online service goes out of business, you can buy another BIP39-compliant device from another manufacturer, and you'll still be fine.

Full disclosure, using BIP39 may slightly reduce the security of your Bitcoin wallet, though the effect is negligible.

Many hardware wallet solutions will allow you to lock the device with a password or biometrics. Using some or all of the security features correctly and keeping your seed phrase safe and secret limits your exposure to Bitcoin loss.

Proprietary vs. Open Source

This information should help you decide what is the best fit for you. Do your own research if you need more than the most basic of descriptions like the ones provided below, or flip a coin if you don't care.

- Proprietary: Some manufacturers create their own devices with their own software solutions. These proprietary devices come with the downside that you have to trust in the company's design skills and motives. The upside is that it can be more challenging for hackers and attackers to find exploits, since they have less information on the software's inner workings. The downside is that proprietary solutions tend to take longer to see bug fixes, as you only have the owner of the software designing, testing, and implementing these fixes. The Ledger Nano X https://shop.ledger.com/products/ledger-backup-pack?r=36a05bea1a87&tracker=HowToOwn Bitcoin is an example of a proprietary hardware wallet.
- Open Source: Other manufacturers create the hardware but rely on open source, freely available software to run the de-

vice. Open source means that every line of code is available for review online. It comes with the downside that its entire programming code is laid bare for anyone to read, making it easier to find exploits. The upside is that there is potentially a vast community of people who all want to see bugs fixed fast. You can also assume there are many eyes on the code to catch and correct bugs, problems, and exploits before someone with bad intentions finds them first. Many programmers pride themselves on finding and fixing bugs in open source software, and it can be quite competitive. A Trezor is an example of a manufacturer of open source hardware wallets. Look up their product line here https://shop.trezor.io/?offer_id=10&aff_id=6003&source=HowToOwnBitcoin

- If open source and proprietary software sound like magic, that's because they are, and you can pick either if you don't have a strong opinion on it. In that case, go with the one whose interface you think will be easier to use, or look for some other feature that is important to you. Or, as stated, flip a coin.

Warning: NEVER use a hardware wallet with a history. No refurbished devices, no used devices, no discount bin devices. ALWAYS buy your hardware wallets directly from the manufacturer. Used, refurbished, or contaminated devices can harbor viruses or malware designed to steal your cryptocurrencies, and there is no one you can cry to when your Bitcoin wallet gets drained. Remember, the city of Troy was happy to accept a giant wooden horse and bring it in through their front gate.

If your hardware wallet is lost or stolen, consider transferring your Bitcoin and other cryptocurrencies from the affected wallet into new secure wallets until you find it. If your hardware wallet was password protected, the chances of your Bitcoin remaining secure are much higher, but don't rely on this safety measure for longer than reasonable.

It's unlikely that anyone will bother with a random hardware wallet; still, expensive and specialized equipment can read the information off a hardware chip memory even if the device is locked with a password.

Do your own research before buying! And have a plan on how you are going to use these wallets before you open their package and initialize them. For example, both Ledger and Trezor optionally support multi-signature wallets. These special Bitcoin wallets require more than one device to access your Bitcoin, which allows you to split up access to your wallet into different geographic locations or require multiple people to create transactions. There are even services that will hold one of your multi-sig shares online so there is one more layer of protection. See Chapter 4.9 Multi-Signature for the benefits and risks involved in using multi-sig. Ledger can also have a hidden wallet if you set it up carefully. That is a rabbit hole for another day, another book, another web search for "two Bitcoin wallets on a Ledger Nano."

You earned:
+60 Risk
+25 Confidence

Continue down this path by reading further or go back to Chapter 4 Subchapter Selection

CHAPTER 4.3
COLD STORAGE - HOME BREW HARDWARE WALLET

If you want to go off the deep end (or need to save a couple of bucks to buy more Satoshis) and don't mind taking on significantly more risk, you can consider one of the many methods to make your own hardware wallet. Options include using a Raspberry Pi, an old mobile phone, an old computer or laptop, etc., and turning it into an offline cryptocurrency hardware wallet. Almost any device with enough processing power (doesn't take much) and a web browser can be converted. Due to the massive number of possibilities and combinations of hardware and software solutions for this, this will be a project you will have to research fully. This chapter is only here as food for thought to get your juices flowing so you can decide if this is the sort of thing you would enjoy doing. When considering the electronics you have lying around for this, you can use the steps in Chapter 4.6 Cold Storage - Paper Wallet - Digital Version if the device has a powerful enough web browser. (You'll just have to test it.)

Warning: Unless you know what you are doing and the risks involved, these devices MUST be taken offline first; remove SIM cards, turn off Wi-Fi, Bluetooth, NFC, etc. This device must NEVER go online—not ever—as long as any of the Bitcoin wallets created or stored on it have any cryptocurrencies stored in them or if they will ever have cryptocurrencies stored in them. Old devices remember things, and a savvy hacker could get your address off a dead phone years later. Even a regular printer can store images of what it prints for years. Famous data hacks were achieved by rescuing old printers and computers out of the dump. When it comes to your tech, stay paranoid, friends.

There are many devices which can be converted to hardware wallets, and there are a host of ways in which this can go horribly wrong. Test your hardware wallet vigorously with small amounts of Bitcoin and the other cryptocurrencies you'll use with it before you ever trust putting in large amounts. Always ensure you have appropriate backups of recovery keys, seed phrases, etc., for every currency you store. Do not keep these recovery methods on the device in case it fails critically. Remember, no one can help you if you lose your private key. No one can assist with Bitcoin recovery if you mess up. If you choose to do this, it's recommended to start with a device that has been completely wiped and restored to its factory defaults before playing around, just in case it has or had viruses and such.

Have fun, and tinker with caution.

You earned:
+100 Risk
+50 Difficulty

Continue down this path by reading further or go back to Chapter 4 Subchapter Selection

CHAPTER 4.4
COLD STORAGE - UNSAFE BUT CONVENIENT HARDWARE WALLET

You can use your current mobile phone as a hardware wallet, even if it does not have a Trusted Execution Environment chipset mentioned in Chapter 4.1 Cold Storage - Hardware Wallet - Smartphone with TEE chip. If your phone does have a Trusted Execution Environment chipset, consider the safety provided by using this chip instead of following the information in this chapter. Chapter 4.3 Cold Storage - Hardware Wallet - Home Brew mentions repurposing an old phone, but that phone should be offline. This chapter talks about using a device you know is at risk because it is online and actively used as a phone.

There are many apps you can install from your phone's app store to custody and manage your Bitcoin. This method probably has the highest risk of any method mentioned in this book, but the potential advantages may warrant the risk in some cases. You are exposed to this risk whenever you enter your private key, seed phrase, or recovery phrase into these apps. Even if you trust the app implicitly, your phone could have a virus, your phone's keyboard app might be monitoring what you type, your camera might be snagging images of the QR codes you scan. This is why it is essential that you only store small amounts of Bitcoin in it or none at all. You might also consider only using temporary Bitcoin wallets with this method. You can follow the steps in Chapter 4.6 Cold Storage - Paper Wallet - Digital Version to learn how to make as many Bitcoin wallets as you like (look for "Bulk Wallet" in the bullet points). Once you have used one of these temporary addresses and removed all of your Bitcoin from them, it might be best to note the addresses as burned so that you never use them again.

Do your research, read the reviews. Find an app that does what you need and seems trustable. Only download these apps from trusted app stores. Know your risk.

You earned:
+250 Risk
+25 Impatience

Continue down this path by reading further or Go Back to Chapter 4 Subchapter Selection

CHAPTER 4.5
COLD STORAGE - SOFTWARE WALLET

Software is available to create and manage your Bitcoin. Some of these software suites can be used on two computers or devices for greater security. Think of how a hardware wallet has two chips inside; one chip is isolated from the internet, which protects your private key, and the other allows for management and creation of transactions. There are software suites which allow you to create this isolated system on two computers or devices. One computer is connected to the internet, while the other is permanently isolated. Alternatively, you can use this type of software with only one device, but this comes with a lot of risks.

The online computer or device gets a limited copy of the Bitcoin wallet containing only the public addresses so you can check your balances and create signable transactions. These transactions can then be transferred to an offline computer or device that also runs the software. This offline device has the private key of your Bitcoin wallet(s), so it is able to sign the transaction. Once the transaction is signed, it can be transferred back to the online computer, where the software can send the signed transaction to the Bitcoin network for verification.

By doing the signing on an offline computer or device, you are able to isolate your Bitcoin wallet from the outside world, assuming the method you use to transfer the transactions back and forth is safe and does not introduce a virus or malware to the offline computer. Typically, clean thumb drives are used (USB drive, flash drive, pen drive). If you know how, you should make sure the offline computer does not automatically load software from the thumb drive when it is detected. Older computer systems had this flaw.

The two free software suites mentioned below are both a bit challenging to learn. You've got to be willing to nerd it out a bit if you want to use these, but if you go down this rabbit hole, they both provide some very interesting tools mostly unavailable with any other method mentioned in this book. If you are not a total nerd, click here to go back to Chapter 4 Subchapter Selection.

Bitcoin Armory is the first option. It is an open source project that many use and has two versions. You can go to https://www.Bitcoinarmory.com/ to find the original project. According to their site, lead of the project was handed over in February 2016, and the hard fork can be found at https://btcarmory.com/

Bitcoin Armory is exceptionally robust, but you need to test the Bitcoin wallets it creates with small amounts of Bitcoin before storing large amounts in them due to being in development. It would be best if you also made backups of your seed phrase in case of failure. Do your own research! There is a chance that—depending on what backup steps you use—you could lose all of your Bitcoin through your own mistakes, a device failure, or if Armory stops as a project. (DYOR!)

To use Armory to its fullest, you may choose to download, install, and run Bitcoin Core from https://Bitcoin.org. If you decide to run a full Bitcoin node, it will be a massive download, taking hours, days, or weeks to complete on some internet connections. Downloading it could easily surpass some internet plans' data limits, incurring high costs and fines from your internet service provider. It uses a lot of hard drive storage and memory as well, so it might not be possible to run it on some devices.

Electrum is another popular software solution which can be found at https://electrum.org. Make sure you use *.org* and not *.com*, as the *.com* site has been reported as a scam (though the *.com* site refutes these claims and seems quite chuffed about it). Electrum Bitcoin Wallet is a lot like Armory, and is also intended for intermediately skilled users. Unlike Armory, Electrum does not require installing and running a Bitcoin Core node, therefore, it does require trust in a third party for accurate on-chain data about your wallets.

Using software solutions like Armory and Electrum come with their own set of complications and risks. As usual, do your own research, use some or all of their security features for any Bitcoin wallets that you would mind losing, and always test your setup with a small amount of Bitcoin before transferring larger amounts into or out of any Bitcoin wallet.

Check Chapter 6.10 Electrum Watch-Only Wallet to see an example of using Electrum's stand-alone app (no install required) to create a watch-only wallet that lets you look at the balances of your Bitcoin wallets without exposing the private keys to anyone. You can also use this to monitor public addresses that you don't own, in case you want to snoop or stay informed for some reason.

You earned:
+50 Difficulty
+30 Nerdiness

Continue down this path by reading further or go back to Chapter 4 Subchapter Selection

CHAPTER 4.6
COLD STORAGE - PAPER WALLET GENERATORS

As mentioned in earlier chapters, you can simply choose a large number within the Bitcoin address range and have yourself a Bitcoin wallet, but who wants to do that? And once you choose a Bitcoin wallet private key, there are complicated equations to calculate your public address from your private key. It's quite mathy to do the equations by hand. To make this much easier, people have created websites which help you choose a private key at random. In addition, they will generate public addresses, QR codes of these addresses, and have other fun and useful wallet-generation tools. If this sounds like something you'd enjoy using, you can easily create a Bitcoin wallet.

This method is called a paper wallet because it was originally designed to be printed or written down on paper, go figure. It does NOT require paper, however! If you have hardware lying around that can do this—like an old laptop or mobile phone—a paper wallet might be more cost-effective than purchasing a Chapter 4.2 Cold Storage - Hardware Wallet - Professional. Paper wallets can be generated by web pages you can download and use offline.

This chapter will focus on using this method to create Bitcoin wallets from scratch using a piece of hardware that can run a web page. Many old (but not too old) smartphones can run the equations to create a paper wallet.

For those of you who have come this far into wonderland, below you'll find one method for creating paper wallets, though it is up to you to discover more methods. Even if this does not sound like something you would be interested in using, going through the first steps and exploring the website can be a good lesson in Bitcoin.

Creating a Paper Wallet

When you create your first Bitcoin paper wallets to play with, you can ignore the Rules of Paranoia for Creating a Paper Wallet listed at the end of this section. While playing with small amounts of Bitcoin and learning how it all works, you don't need to take all of the offline precautions. These experimental addresses should not be used once you are done playing with them, though. Once you are ready to make a more permanent Bitcoin wallet, consider your risks when dealing with any significant amount of Bitcoin, and yes, be that paranoid. As always, Do Your Own Research.

One trusted method to create a paper wallet is to use https://www.bitaddress.org. This chapter will focus on this tool, but you can use other similar ones if you are careful and do your due diligence. Another website which does the same thing is https://walletgenerator.net. This website is much the same as https://www.bitaddress.org, but it also allows you to create many other cryptocurrency paper wallets, like Ethereum. As mentioned, there is a lot of risk when using this method. Be wary!

These instructions are based on version 3.3.0 of https://bitaddress.org.

1. Go to https://bitaddress.org on any trusted online device with a web browser.
2. Ignore any dots popping up on the screen or the % numbers increasing for now (if they show up).
3. At the bottom of the page on the left, there is a link to download the GitHub repository ZIP file. Download it and extract the HTML file.
    a. Alternatively, you can use your web browser to download or save the page directly from https://www.bitaddress.org, just as it is. Everything needed for this web page to work is self-contained in the single HTML file. Even the graphics are embedded.

4. Next, you may need to transfer this saved web page onto the offline device you plan to create your Bitcoin wallets on.
   a. If you are making Bitcoin addresses for experimentation, learning, or don't need the usually necessary security of an offline device, you can skip this step (#4). Be aware, though, that all addresses created through this method on an online device should be considered compromised.
   b. If you downloaded the web page on the device you plan to create your Bitcoin wallets on, take the device offline and never connect it again. It might be advisable to go into Wi-Fi settings and make the device forget all of the Wi-Fi routers it knows. Turn off Wi-Fi, Bluetooth, NFC, etc. Remove the SIM card and set the device to aeroplane mode if this is an option. Be paranoid.
   c. If the saved web page is NOT on the device you plan to take offline to create your Bitcoin wallets, find a safe way to copy the saved page from bitaddress.org to that device. Usually via a thumb drive or some other portable storage device.
5. Make sure to use the website's verification process at the bottom of the page to ensure you have an unaltered, uncorrupted web page.
6. Once you have verified the saved page on an offline device, you can now create as many paper wallets as you'd like!

To make Bitcoin wallets:

1. Open the verified, saved web page on a completely sandboxed, offline device. If you are properly paranoid, ensure no one can see your screen, including through webcams of any kind, security cameras, mobile phone cameras, and other video or photo equipment that connects to the internet.
2. As soon as the web page loads, it uses your mouse's movement—or text typed into the box—to create a unique

generation seed. This one-time, behind-the-scenes seed is used to generate as many addresses as you'd like. This seed generation is used due to computers' inability to choose truly random numbers. Moving your mouse around is sufficient enough to create a random-seeming number for this purpose.

    a. If your device has a mouse, wiggle it around until the percentages get to a hundred.

    b. If your device has no mouse, you can type random numbers and letters into the text box until the percentages get to a hundred. This is less random, but good enough.

3. Once at a hundred percent—if your device has enough processing power and memory—the web page should generate a private key and a set of public addresses for you. There is no need to store all of the Bitcoin wallets created; they are expendable if unused. You must properly record the ones you plan to use by writing them down, printing them, saving to a thumb drive, etc. You could generate twenty addresses and only use one; don't worry about accidentally creating extra wallets.

Congratulations! You've made your first Bitcoin wallet. This wallet is not necessarily the best Bitcoin wallet for all situations. Read below to see more options. For example, if you plan to print your wallet on paper (versus writing it down), you may consider using one of the BIP38 encrypted methods listed below for more security. Click the green tabs at the top of the web page to create Bitcoin wallets using different methods.

Types of Bitcoin wallets you can create on https://bitaddress.org's version 3.3.0 web page:

- **Single Wallet:** Creates one single wallet with a public address, private keys, and their corresponding QR codes to scan. Since there is no BIP38 encryption for this page, it is not advised to print these addresses.

- **Paper Wallet:** These are fancy-looking Bitcoin wallets you can print and give as gifts. It provides the gift recipient with the public and private keys of the wallet, along with the QR codes. These can be BIP38 encrypted, but the recipient will need the BIP38 passphrase to spend the Bitcoin from these papers. It might be worth writing it on the paper in this case. The point of using BIP38 on these Bitcoin wallets is to prevent exposure when printing on a suspicious network and printer. You may consider keeping a backup print (and the BIP38 passphrase) of these wallets in case the recipient loses the paper.
- **Bulk Wallet:** It allows the creation of bulk lists of addresses. These can be BIP38 encrypted. Example uses are:
    - o Large lists of wallet addresses can be used to receive online payments as a business. Your website can be coded to provide a random public address from the generated list for each customer. This obfuscates information about how often and how much money your company is receiving.
    - o If you want a lot of addresses to spread your Bitcoin around so it's not all in one address. This can increase complication, security, anonymity, etc.
    - o If you want backup addresses to use on unsecured sites or apps. This would give you as many throwaway Bitcoin wallets as you might need. Don't want your moochy friend knowing how much Bitcoin you have received in your lifetime? Give them one of the throwaway addresses to pay you in, then all they will see are their own transactions if they ever check. But if you transfer these Bitcoin into your main address, a savvy, moochy friend can follow the Bitcoin trail on-chain and still see your other transactions. You can keep the Bitcoin in that wallet until you spend them

or transfer them onto an exchange to help obfuscate your other addresses.

  o Creating a bunch of addresses so you don't have to pull out your sandboxed offline device every time you need a new one. You can copy/paste the public keys and save them to a computer that is online with limited risk. You'll only need to pull out the sandboxed computer when trying to access Bitcoin in these addresses.

- **Brain Wallet:** This page allows you to type a phrase, string of words, or sentence and create an address from that.
  o This method is not advisable except for cases where you need to bring your Bitcoin with you and can't trust anything but your own brain.
  o You must remember every single character, capitalization, spacing, punctuation, etc. It must be precise; it must be very long. Consider typing in a long sentence with no capitalization, spacing, or punctuation. Example: ireallylikethisbitcoinbookandwanttolikeand comment or ihopeborderpatroldoesnottorturethisout ofme
  o The text strings used for the passphrase should be very long; not long like a password for your email, but long enough that no one can guess it.
  o Once you arrive at a safe location with your brain wallet, you can repeat the process of going to bitaddress.org and typing in this long phrase. If you typed it precisely, without a single mistake, the site will generate the same Bitcoin wallet for you again so you can access your Bitcoin. Make sure you do this on an offline device if you have the option. (The random seed created by moving your mouse has no effect on the Brain Wallet tab.)

- **Vanity Wallets:** This is an advanced feature. It is not recommended unless you already understand it. Hint: it has something to do with creating millions of Bitcoin wallets until you find a keyword hidden away in the public address. This way, you could have a public address that has your name or nickname within it. The longer the word or words you are looking for, the longer it will take to find one. Even with powerful computers, this can take months or years, depending on the complexity. There are companies you can pay to find you a vanity wallet, but you are then trusting them to not steal your Bitcoin, since they will also know your private key. Don't bother with these services.

- **Split Wallets:** These are also called multi-sig or multi-signature Bitcoin wallets. This tab can create Bitcoin wallets that don't have single points of failure. These Bitcoin wallets are encoded in a way that access to the Bitcoin wallet is broken into shares. Depending on how you create these, you can require that either all of the shares or just a portion of them be used to access the Bitcoin wallet. To remove Bitcoin from the Bitcoin wallet, you would need two or more shares to sign the transaction. More on this topic in Chapter 4.9 Multi-Signature

- **Dice-Rolled Bitcoin Wallet:** On the bottom of the Wallet Details tab, you'll find instructions on using dice to create a Bitcoin wallet if you still don't trust the website's mouse/typing seed creation. Just remember, if you are working on a corrupted version of bitaddress.org, this method won't protect you from attack either. This method is more of a point of interest than anything else. There are ways of crunching the numbers yourself, though, if you do your own research. This might be the very bottom of the rabbit hole for even the numberphile nerds out there.

- **Wallet Details:** This page will allow you to enter a private key and optional BIP38 encrypted private key. This tab calculates some of the useful addresses from the private key you entered. Remember to only use this page on a fully offline device.

Note: If you use an online service to check the status of your on-chain Bitcoin transactions for an address, only the version of the public address you used will show results for some sites. For example, if you sent Bitcoin to the Public Address, forget, then do a search using the Public Address Compressed, it will most likely not show your transaction.

Once you have created the addresses you need, there are a few things you can do with them safely while staying digital. Even though it's called a paper wallet, you don't have to write anything down or even print anything out as long as your private keys are stored securely somewhere (with backups somewhere else). If you do print, it is recommended that you only print addresses generated using BIP38 encryption. This way, if the printed page is compromised in transit or your printer becomes compromised, the encrypted addresses will be useless without the BIP38 passphrase. Ensure you don't forget or lose your BIP38 passphrase, or the Bitcoin will be lost forever. You could consider the pros and cons of writing your BIP38 passphrase on the printed paper or writing a note that will remind you what the passphrase is. You could also keep the passphrase completely separate as an added layer of protection. Don't make it so difficult that your beneficiaries can't figure it out!

Since you are using a sandboxed, offline device, printing might not be an option anyway. Many operating systems will allow you to create PDFs from the print menu, and these can be safely transported via a thumb drive to an online computer if the Bitcoin wallets were created with BIP38. Due to printer failures or formatting issues, you should verify that every single character of every address was printed correctly and fully. Poor formatting could cut off the last characters of your private key without you noticing. Depending on the fonts and Bitcoin wallet formats, all the keys may look complete, but one of them could be cut off.

It is safe to copy/paste all of the public addresses (notice it says public addresses, not private keys) to a text file and store them less securely. It is the private keys you must guard and keep safe. Add notes to each if you need to remember what kind they are, or notes to help remind you what private key goes with what public address.

One benefit of the Bulk Wallet tab is that they are numbered. You can create fifty or so BIP38 encrypted addresses then copy/paste them into a text file. Add any notes you need, then save this file twice. You could name one file *Public* and one file *Private*. In the Public file, you can then go and CAREFULLY delete all of the private keys from each line of text, leaving behind the numbered public addresses. This file can then be loaded onto a thumb drive and safely moved to your online device. Note that you are not copying the Private file which contains all of the private keys to the thumb drive. You should consider some form of archival backup for the Private file, as you don't want one point of failure.

We will talk about how to get Bitcoin out of paper storage in Chapter 3.6 Cold Storage - Paper Wallet - Digital Version.

Once you have your files created, you can store your private keys in many ways, but you need to make sure that whatever method(s) you choose has a very high probability of lasting physically and staying safe and secure from villains, bullies, moochy friends, and pirates.

Things to consider:

- All electronics fail over time. Make multiple backups, preferably on different brands of devices. Store them according to the manufacturer's instructions. Some devices are better suited for long-term storage or archiving than others. DYOR.
- Consider theft, fire, and water damage when storing your keys.
- Don't hide your Bitcoin secrets so well that your beneficiaries can't recover them if you become unavailable. If you trust the person or persons you want to leave your Bitcoin to when you have no use for it anymore, consider confiding in and training them on how to get to your super-secret, encrypted, hidden stash of Bitcoin wallets. Read more about this risk in Chapter 6.9 Excess Paranoia.
- The more locations you store your private keys in, the more risk of exposure.

- The fewer locations you store your private keys in, the more risk of damage or loss.
- Storing your BIP38 passphrases in a different location from your private keys will increase security but make it more challenging to get to your Bitcoin in an emergency if you don't have them memorized.
- Don't store unencrypted private keys online. To be safe, you probably shouldn't store BIP38 encrypted addresses online either, especially if there is any chance of your passphrase becoming compromised or if you're storing multiple BIP38 encrypted Bitcoin wallets together encrypted with the same passphrase.
- Test, test, test. Make sure you did everything correctly by using a small amount of Bitcoin with throwaway addresses you made following the exact same method as the ones you plan to keep. (But maybe use a different passphrase for the BIP38 encryption.)
- Be paranoid. Be careful who and what you trust. Being your own bank comes with a certain level of responsibility.
- Try to avoid single points of failure caused by the complexity of your method.
- Try to avoid single points of failure where someone can gain access to your private keys or seed phrases or other information with ease.

Rules of Paranoia When Creating a Paper Wallet:

Rule 1: Be extra paranoid with any Bitcoin private key in which you plan to put sizable amounts of Bitcoin you care about losing.

Rule 2: Be even a little more paranoid. Create all Bitcoin wallets on an offline device you will never put online as long as the Bitcoin wallets created there still have any Bitcoin in them or will have Bitcoin in the future.

Rule 3: Be paranoid enough to cover all cameras; webcams, mobile phones, security cameras, even some televisions have cameras for

Skype. If you intend to take this seriously, why not take it very seriously? Assume everyone is trying to get to your Bitcoin and that all of your online-capable devices are infected with horrible Bitcoin-stealing viruses.

Rule 4: Use trusted methods and do your own research. Try and figure out how someone might attack your Bitcoin. For example, if you use an offline web page to generate your Bitcoin wallet, consider the possibility that a corrupted download of this trusted offline Bitcoin wallet generator might actually be feeding you predesignated addresses known to the attacker, and not actually generating anything.

Rule 5: Be paranoid and use whatever verification methods the trusted tools you use offer.

Rule 6: Someone is always out to get your Bitcoin.

Rule 7: If you can't handle being paranoid or your risk aversion is high or you are trying to cold-store more Bitcoin than you can handle losing, consider using methods from Chapter 2.

Rule 8: Seriously, if you are in a life-and-death bid to escape with your family across borders, consider using a method that allows you to use BIP39 seed phrases or a brain Bitcoin wallet. More information in this chapter. The chances that you'll remember your seed phrase or brain Bitcoin wallet phrase are much higher than memorizing a Bitcoin Wallet alphanumeric private key. Try to make sure more than one competent, trusted adult knows the phrase, and try not to get into any situation where someone else might torture it out of you.

Rule 9: Read more about Bitcoin paranoia in Chapter 6.9 Excess Paranoia

You earned:

+ 500 Nerdiness

+ 500 Difficulty

+ 250 Confidence (Hopefully the step-by-step process helps)

Continue down this path by reading further or go back to Chapter 4 Subchapter Selection

CHAPTER 4.7
COLD STORAGE - PHYSICALLY ARCHIVING KEYS AND SEEDS

If you bought a hardware wallet or followed the instructions in Chapter 4.6 Cold Storage - Paper Wallet - Digital Version, you should have a seed phrase or private key that you need to back up and store safely. There are many methods to back up numbers or phrases, all with differing levels of complexity, security, and redundancy.

You can print, write, or inscribe your seed phrase or Bitcoin private key on many materials. You can also store it digitally (offline, hopefully). Some will last longer than others. Some are more durable than others. There are specialty papers and pens of archival quality that could last much longer than your average printing or writing materials. You could even store them on metal, like engraving a titanium sheet for longevity and durability. This chapter is not so much a how-to as just thoughts and warnings.

- Never buy Bitcoin wallets that are already inscribed with a preassigned private key. There are companies that will sell you metal or paper business cards with a private key of their choosing, or a metal plate inscribed with a private key. You have to trust them not to have kept a copy! Not your keys, not your Bitcoin!
- Never send your private key out for anyone to inscribe it for you.
- Never give out your private key for any reason until you feel you have a perfect understanding of Bitcoin and its risks. There are very few scenarios where giving out your private key is a good idea!
- Whoever has your private keys owns your Bitcoin!

"Your keys, your Bitcoin. Not your keys, not your Bitcoin."
—Andreas Antonopoulos

There are products out there that give you a set of metal letters and numbers to place into a special, physical metal Bitcoin wallet. They claim to be waterproof and fireproof. If you want to go a little more medieval, you can buy metal stamps and a titanium sheet. Together with a hammer, you can stamp every case-sensitive letter and number of your keys and BIP38 passphrases into the metal. Stamps and a metal sheet might be more cost-effective if you are storing many keys and seeds. To save time, you only need the first four letters of each seed word (record a blank at the end of three letter words). This can be tedious and subject to human error; be careful and remember to test your archival private keys, BIP38 passphrases, and seed phrases in an offline and secure manner before adding large amounts of Bitcoin to archival, paper, or metal Bitcoin wallets.

Some tungsten has a maximum working temperature of 1300 degrees Celsius. Typical house fires can exceed 1500 degrees. A tungsten sheet in a fireproof safe can improve your chances of its survival. Fireproof safes are not fireproof, but they massively extend the amount of time the contents inside stay below a specific temperature. Placing your archival backups inside of a fireproof insulated bag inside of a fireproof safe can increase your chances of success further. If you are storing electronics as a backup method, you'll need to be careful to put them in a dry, waterproof, airtight container and include some quality desiccant to prevent condensation from slowly destroying your electronics. This includes thumb drives, computer parts, professional hardware wallets, hard drives, memory cards, or self-made hardware wallets. Even in arid climates, fireproof safes can slowly destroy electronics and other metal items that are not protected thanks to condensation from minor temperature fluctuations. There are rechargeable desiccant products that are plugged in periodically outside of the safe. One example is Eva-Dry Wireless Mini Dehumidifier, White (E-333).

Consider keeping copies of your keys in more than one location in case of a worst-case scenario. These locations could be two secure places in your home or two different geographic locations.

Review Chapter 6.9 Excess Paranoia and Chapter 4.9 Multi-Signature for more information about maximizing security.

Consider a tungsten Bitcoin wallet Turducken (this is not a thing; it's a joke): place your tungsten sheet with engraved seed phrase into a fire-resistant insulating bag, then put it in your fireproof safe. You could then hire fire-retardant security trolls to patrol the perimeter of your fire-resistant underground bomb shelter...hold up. Too paranoid? Just the tungsten sheet in the fireproof bag is probably good enough for most. Being able to store it in a safe could be a bonus. Choosing whether to secure it in a safe or hiding it is up to you.

Just a reminder, if you are storing a BIP39-compliant seed phrase, you only need the first four letters of each word. The BIP39 list of English words does not have any two words in it where the first four letters match. There are three-letter words on the list, however, so remember to record a space as the fourth letter of these.

You earned:
+ 55 Nerdiness
+ 100 Risk

Continue down this path by reading further or go back to Chapter 4 Subchapter Selection

CHAPTER 4.8
COLD STORAGE - PAPER WALLET
- WITHDRAWING BITCOIN

Making a paper wallet is simple. Safely taking the Bitcoin out can be a bit trickier. Assuming you have your Bitcoin private key, you have a few choices if you want to be overly cautious.

- **The easiest way:** Use a trusted exchange, website, or service which allows importing and sweeping of private keys. http://exchange.Blockchain.com is an example of such a website. The smartphone app called Mycelium is another option. *Sweeping* means that the software will check the balance of an address then empty it into another Bitcoin wallet, like the one the website provides for you or one of your own. On some of these platforms, you can transfer directly from one wallet to another you have the public address for, like your hardware wallet or paper wallets. There is a risk of a man-in-the-middle attack, where your transfer gets sent to a thief's address, but as long as you are using a trusted site/app on a trusted device and transferring your Bitcoin to an address you have the sole control of, the risks may be limited. Be careful if you use these kinds of methods for Bitcoin you can't afford to lose.

  Example: Once you have an account on http://exchange. Blockchain.com and you've logged in, explore the menus to find "Wallets and Addresses" in settings. Here, you can import Bitcoin private keys. When you do, http://exchange. Blockchain.com will ask you if you would like to sweep the address. If you agree, this will transfer all of the Bitcoin to your http://exchange.Blockchain.com Bitcoin wallet.

Pros
- Very easy.
- Very Fast.
- Low learning curve.

Cons
- You have to trust the exchange, website, or service with your Bitcoin.
- You have to be using a device clean of viruses and malware.
- You should probably stop using the Bitcoin wallet that you import. Let the exchange, website, or service sweep the address and transfer all of your Bitcoin to their online Bitcoin wallet, then take note that you will not trust that old paper wallet anymore. If you also don't trust the online wallet, transfer your Bitcoin out of it to a wallet you do own and trust ASAP. You'll incur double the gas fees doing this double transfer, though.
- Loss of anonymity, if you care about such things. If your Bitcoin wallet had anonymity, it would probably be lost. All on-chain transactions like this risk revealing who you are to the authorities and chainalytics companies. Funds you transfer out of the exchange, website, or service may be tracked as having been owned by you, and anyone can go back and potentially see where you received your Bitcoin from if that address is also known.
- **The somewhat easy way:** Use a trusted online app or program to take all of your Bitcoin out of your address and send it directly to another Bitcoin paper wallet. You can move it all to another address or multiple addresses that are still secret. It's essential, however, that all of the Bitcoin is removed and moved somewhere safe. Mark the old Bitcoin private key as burned, and never use it again. Assume this Bitcoin wallet has been compromised.

Pros

- Easy.
- Fast.
- Relatively low risk overall. Especially if you use trusted apps and programs with a virus-free trusted device.
- Suitable for long-term hodling, but not as convenient for regular use.
- Lower gas fees if the program can transfer directly from the address it is sweeping to the Bitcoin wallet you would like it in.

Cons

- Most risk of someone stealing your Bitcoin, and most risk of you making a mistake and losing your own Bitcoin.
- You have to abandon this Bitcoin wallet and move to a new one, adding to the risk of making a mistake.
- Depending on how you do this, you may have to temporarily hold this Bitcoin on a service or exchange while working with it.
- This could add to the gas fees you pay, depending on how you do this.
- Loss of anonymity. If your Bitcoin wallet had any anonymity, it would be lost. All on-chain transactions like this risk revealing who you are to the authorities. Funds you transfer out of the exchange, website, or service may be tracked as having been owned by you, and anyone can go back and potentially see where you received your Bitcoin from if that address is known.

Notes

- Spreading your Bitcoin into multiple addresses from the start can limit your risk exposure if something goes wrong.

- **Example:** there are apps which let you enter your private key and send all or a portion of that address's Bitcoin to another address. These apps usually promise that the private key is not kept by them. Even if you believe them, you know the risks; your phone could have a virus, its keyboard app could be monitoring what you type, the camera could be snagging images of the QR codes you scan. Of course, these other apps that are also on your phone say they are benign and only take our information for research purposes. Still, if you are down here in Chapter 4 I Can Be My Own Bank, there is a chance you have a healthy amount of skepticism and paranoia, and don't trust these apps even a little bit.
- This is a great example of a use for the Bulk wallets you can create in Chapter 4.6 Cold Storage - Paper Wallet - Digital Version. If you don't plan to move your Bitcoin often, and especially if you have your massive amounts of cold-stored Bitcoin spread out into many addresses, this method can work well and somewhat reduce risks.

- **More complicated way:** Using an offline computer or device like the one described in Chapter 4.5 Cold Storage - Software Wallet, you can sign transactions somewhat safely. You create the transactions on a trusted online device without the device knowing the private key. Then you transfer this transaction's file to your offline device. It will allow you to sign the file for transmission to the Bitcoin network from the online device.

Pros
- One of the safest ways to manage your Bitcoin on your own terms.
- It does not require a paper wallet, but you can use one with this method.

- The offline device can create a special online Bitcoin wallet that your online device can use to check your Bitcoin wallets' balances without exposing the private keys to theft.
- You can sweep your own addresses instead of relying on third-party online services.

Cons

- Requires trusting the software suite you use.
- Requires moving files back and forth between your online and offline devices, probably with a thumb drive.
- In theory, this method could expose your offline computer to malicious software during the many file transfers.
- Loss of anonymity. Total anonymity is never a guarantee with on-chain Bitcoin transactions.
- This method is for advanced users only.

You earned:
+150 Understanding
+40 Nerdiness

Continue down this path by reading further or go back to Chapter 4 Subchapter Selection

CHAPTER 4.9
MULTI-SIGNATURE

Multi-sig is an encryption, security, redundancy, and access management method that enables you to split a Bitcoin wallet into multiple parts. Each part of a multi-sig wallet is called a share. Each share can partially sign a transaction. Once enough shares have signed the transaction, it can be submitted to the Bitcoin network. Multi-sig can greatly enhance your security by making it difficult or impossible for one single person to have full access to a Bitcoin wallet. You may be trying to prevent a thief from gaining access to your Bitcoin by splitting it up, or you may be working with other people and want to share the ownership and control of the Bitcoin for trust or security reasons.

Multi-sig wallets can require any number of shares to gain access to the Bitcoin wallet. You can have a wallet that requires two out of two shares (2/2) to gain access. You could keep one share and put another in the safe of a trusted family member. This makes getting to your Bitcoin more difficult, as you would need to travel to or contact this family member to get the other share to sign a transaction. This layer of security also adds a layer of risk. What if either of the two keys is lost or destroyed? In this case, you have doubled your chances for single points of failure! Solving this dilemma is where it gets interesting.

Multi-sig also allows a fractional shares system. This is where the number of shares required to access your Bitcoin is less than the total number of shares. A 2/5 system would require any two of the five shares to fully sign a transaction.

Both Ledger's and Trezor's professional hardware wallets allow the creation of multi-sig wallets. You can also make one yourself by using the steps in Chapter 4.6 Cold Storage - Paper Wallet - Digital Version. There are websites mentioned below that also support working with certain hardware wallets. These websites will custody one of your shares for you for backup or security. If you want to hold Bitcoin using multi-sig, you need to research and test your solution before adding any significant amount of Bitcoin to it. Multi-sig adds a whole new layer of complication and risk while being tailored to prevent other risks. Pros and Cons.

Consider these factors when deciding how many shares to create, how many will be required for signing, and how you want to distribute them, store them, and protect them. There are many more things to consider; these are just starting points.

- Every situation is different. There is no correct fits-all solution. Multi-sig might not even be the correct solution for you!
- Giving identical shares to each of your trusted relatives would help prevent them from gaining access by teaming up against you. Doing this, though, requires more careful management of the remaining shares. This reduces diversity.
- Giving different shares to each of your trusted relatives also has benefits. If you trust them enough, it would let them work together to recover your funds if you were incapacitated or unavailable. This would increase diversity while increasing risk in some cases.
- Keeping less shares than the minimum for yourself, but having a service or trusted person, can make it so that home invaders or thieves can't directly access your Bitcoin if they were to obtain your shares.
- If you are sharing control of Bitcoin among multiple people, requiring all shares for a signature creates a risk if a member of the group is incapacitated, arrested, or otherwise unavailable or unwilling to cooperate.
- There are services which will assist in signing transactions for you once you provide them with one or more shares of your multi-sig. This adds another layer of action required to get to your funds. In a 3/5 system, for example, you could control two, the service could control one, and you would have two others to distribute to trusted relatives. You could then put

the service's share in your will with instructions so your family could recover your Bitcoin, but you wouldn't need to bother pulling out your sealed last will and testament every time you want to make a transaction. Example services are:
  o https://unchained-capital.com
  o https://blockstream.com/green
  o https://keys.casa
- Look at a very short list of the risks of overcomplication in Chapter 6.9 Excess Paranoia.
- It's usually best to make sure there is no single point of failure. In most cases, it may be best to require less than a 100 percent of the shares for signing transactions. A 2/2 multi-sig—where you have one and a service has the other— would go badly if that service fails you or you lose your share.
- In case you haven't seen it in the book yet, DYOR! Do your own research. Multi-sig requires careful planning and failure prevention. When you control or custody your own Bitcoin, you take on all of the risks of being your own bank, and there is no one to help you if you mess it up!
- **TEST, TEST, TEST** your multi-sig, then TEST it again. Then try to think of EVERY failure scenario that could make you lose your Bitcoin forever. You have to be OK with the risks you discover and the ones you don't know about if you want to use multi-sig.

WARNING: Recovery of multi-sig shares is not intuitive. If you have a 2/3 multi-sig, you only need two shares to sign a transaction, but you need ALL THREE (100%) of the shares' recovery keys/seeds to recover a lost share. If you still have access to 2/3 shares to sign one last transaction (but lack at least one recovery key), create a new multi-sig wallet and transfer your balance into it. It is usually best to keep each share's recovery seed with it; at a minimum, don't keep all of the recovery seeds in the same place unless it is extremely secure.

Be creative. Be smart. Be careful.

Don't be too creative, though. Overcomplicating multi-sig is bad. If you want someone to be the beneficiary of your Bitcoin, make sure they are fully aware of and trained on how to use your system. Research! Test! Test again! Realize that in ten years (probably ten days if you overcomplicate it), you might not remember how to get your Bitcoin. Only make it as complex as necessary.

Now, let's go crazy with examples.

Let's say you want to distribute your Bitcoin wallet to three locations for security, but you don't trust any one person with your Bitcoin. You could create a 2/3 split multi-sig Bitcoin wallet, then distribute the shares to three different locations. If one location is destroyed, lost, or compromised, you would only need the remaining two shares to gain access to your Bitcoin. If two shares (and their recovery keys/seeds) are destroyed, lost, or compromised, you are completely screwed. In case of a home invasion, a thief would have little use of one share. The risk here is if the two people you entrusted with shares get together without you, they have access to your Bitcoin.

Alternately, you could create a 2/5 split Bitcoin wallet, and include one of the shares in your last will and testament with instructions. You keep two shares for yourself and give out the remaining two to trusted beneficiaries. This way, any one person with a share and access to your last will and testament could recover your Bitcoin. Again, there is a risk that someone named in the will knows what they have, then convinces another beneficiary to give them their share. Then, they could get to your Bitcoin without the will. You can prevent this if you are careful and mathematical. You could give both people the same key so they can't work together, or you could make sure that the number of shares the will has is greater than the number of beneficiaries, like a 3/5 split. This gives two shares to the will, one share to you, then one share each to your two beneficiaries. If the will is destroyed for some reason, you can get the two beneficiaries' shares to regain access to your Bitcoin wallet.

In another scenario, say you want to own Bitcoin jointly with one or more people—perhaps as part of a business—but don't want to entrust control to any one person who might be tempted or coerced to run off with everyone's Bitcoin. You can do a split Bitcoin wallet for the number of people involved. It is best to use a fractional multi-sig and require less than a 100 percent of the shares for signing. Requiring 100 percent creates multiple single points of failure if one of the shares is destroyed, lost, compromised, a shareholder dies, or is somehow made unavailable. Requiring 100 percent would also allow any one person to blackmail the group for access to the Bitcoin by refusing to cooperate.

What if you don't trust yourself not to go to Vegas and blow it all if your Bitcoin doubles or triples in value? See chapter 6.4 Don't Bet the Farm. You could make a 2/3 Bitcoin wallet and give out a share to two people you trust to tell Drunk You "NO!" There may be good services out there that will not only allow you to entrust them with one of your shares for security, but would also put a timer limit on signing transactions. This way, you would have to request a transaction well ahead of time, preventing you from panic selling your hodl and preventing thieves from forcing your hand quickly. This website could give you one or more warnings by email or text that a transaction has been requested so you can act if the transaction is not an authorized one.

You earned:
+50 Understanding
+50 Confidence

Continue down this path by reading further or go back to Chapter 4 Subchapter Selection

CHAPTER 4.10
STAKING

Surprise! This chapter has nothing to do with keeping wooden stakes in your house to fight off vampires who want to suck the Bitcoin out of your wallet. Also, you won't need steak sauce for this chapter.

There are altcoins and other systems where you can stake (store or lend) your cryptocurrencies and gain something in return. This is called staking. It's the same as when you give your money to a bank. You are staking your money with them, and they give you interest on your deposit.

You may find an altcoin which allows you to temporarily stake your Bitcoin and receive an interest rate for letting them borrow your coins. There are services where you can stake your Bitcoin to take out a loan. Some innovative ideas are being tested in the DeFi space in Chapter 5.4 DeFi. Staking could give you access to some benefit if you stake a certain amount of Bitcoin with them. For example, many staking projects allow users with minimum balances staked to vote on the future of the project.

As a crazy fictitious example, there could be a service which lets you borrow any bike throughout a city from a bike-share program as long as you keep X number of Bitcoin or a token they invented called Bike-Coin staked with them as collateral. If you damage or lose their bike, a smart contract could handle the insurance claim when the bike you didn't check back in passes its return period.

It should be obvious by this point in the book that there are a host of risks associated with giving control and access of your private keys to a staking service or altcoin. But technically, staking your Bitcoin is also a place you can store it and get a benefit in return. Do your own research! DYOR!

You earned:

+20 Difficulty

+20 Vocabulary

Read more about steaks, errr...staking in Chapter 5.2 Types of Alt-coins: Stake Coins

Continue down this path by reading further or go back to Chapter 4 Subchapter Selection

CHAPTER 5
ALTCOINS INTRO

Altcoins refer to all of the cryptocurrencies and tokens that are not Bitcoin. (Though some consider Ethereum to be the one other exception, others consider it to be an altcoin.) There can be as many altcoins as humankind can imagine. This is both wonderful and terrifying, making altcoins an exciting and dangerous world. The altcoin space is the Wild West of the digital world; there are visionaries, prospectors, and thieves. Some altcoins are massive projects with huge market caps; others are tiny equivalents of penny stocks. There's money to be made—or lost. There is very little regulation now, and surely a lot of regulation is coming. Beware!

It is strongly recommended to do your own research on every altcoin you dabble in. Many altcoins are built on—or rely upon—other altcoins. Research those, too. Even if your best friend tells you that a certain altcoin is the most fantastic opportunity ever and it can't fail, and they have charts to prove it, do your own research. Altcoins and tokens can be created with no oversight, and are often created without an endgame in mind. Some coins which were so obviously Ponzi schemes they might as well have been called musical chair coins have been developed. Some of these schemes openly admitted their intent to be a Ponzi. It is effortless to lose a lot of money fast in the altcoin world, even on legitimate coins and tokens.

Altcoins do not have to be decentralized like Bitcoin, and many are not. One of Bitcoin's greatest fundamental values is that it is decentralized, but this shoe does not fit on every other coin and token. There is also value in knowing that a huge company is behind the token, forging the way through this new landscape of digital currencies with a purpose, goal, and oversight. Bitcoin has no point of contact to help recover lost Bitcoin, but a centrally controlled altcoin can have such customer support if it is designed that way. Altcoins not being decentralized also leads to risk; unscrupulous creators of an altcoin or token can pump and dump a coin, walking away with all of the money; this has happened more than once. (It's shameful how many times it has happened.) Some of the pump and dump schemes looked very legitimate until the second their coins dropped to 0.0000000 value.

Since the makers of a coin or token can retain some or total control of their product, it is possible for some non-decentralized altcoins to add more coins or tokens any time without warning, devaluing your coins or tokens. This is both good and bad, and can be an important fundamental of some coins. Unlimited coin creation can balance their product as it grows in market value, or can enable them to keep the price or some aspect of the coin linked to some other outside factor. The flip side of this is that the controllers of a crypto can burn coins or tokens, permanently destroying access to them to increase the value of their coin or maintain a reasonable market growth.

Many coins launch with familiar brand names backing them, or which seem like they have great futures, but the makers of the coins and tokens have no clue what they will do with them down the road. Often, the makers are open about that fact. A good salesperson could market the heck out of a worthless coin with their vision of its future but with no actual business plan. You should be aware before you invest. Do your own research. Just because your best friend Bob's friend told him that some coin starting with an *X* was the best coin ever and the price charts are going mad, it does not mean it is safe or wise to invest in it. On the other hand, go wild! Have some fun, take some risks, put some pocket change into a brand-new coin, cross your fingers, and hope it goes BOOM...the good BOOM, not the BOOM-in-your-face BOOM. Never gamble or invest more than you can afford to lose. Stay smart, stay safe.

This book will briefly describe a sampling of various types of coins and tokens. Be aware that a coin/token may start in one category but someday transform into another. Most of the examples below are basic, and they need to be; there are so many variations on each type of coin that it would mire the text to make these examples all-inclusive.

You earned:
+150 Risk
+25 Vocabulary

CHAPTER 5
SUBCHAPTER SELECTION

(Don't tally these points. They're here to help you choose which subchapter is best for you.)

Chapter 5.1 Types of Altcoins: Work Coins
Bitcoin, Ethereum 1, etc.
+100 Work

Chapter 5.2 Types of Altcoins: Stake Coins
Ethereum 2.0, etc.
+100 Stake
-0 Steak

Chapter 5.3 Types of Altcoins: Non-Fungible
Collectable cryptos?
+100 Gaming
+100 Collections
+100 Fan Base

Chapter 5.4 DeFi
The Wild West of crypto: fortunes, fame, and death.
+100 Wild
+100 Wild
+100 West

Chapter 5.5 Oh Yeah, and There Are Proof of...
So many, so confusing, so interesting, much wow, Dogecoin.
+Infinite Possibilities

Oh, risks sound scary. I better read about that before I look into what altcoins are, now that you have me worried.
Oh no, how bad is it, really?

No. No. Don't tell me, I can't bear it.
Ok. Fine. Tell me.

Skip to Chapter 6 Risks and Everything Else
+100 Anxiety
+100 Preparedness

CHAPTER 5.1
TYPES OF ALTCOINS: WORK COINS

Proof-of-work coins and tokens—like Bitcoin or original Ethereum—use complicated math equations to slow the system down. Hard work, for no reason, seems counter-intuitive, but it is what secures the network for these coins. This security stems from math reasons or something equally magical.

It's sort of how the QWERTY typewriter layout was designed to slow typists down so they wouldn't get their keys stuck from typing too fast when they used their old-timey typewriters. (If you don't know what QWERTY is, try typing QWERTY on your computer keyboard.) Bitcoin's complex math slows the whole system enough to make sure its "keys" don't get stuck, pun intended. Although it seems like easy work, and quick transactions would be much better than complicated slower equations, in some cryptographic situations like Bitcoin, faster is not necessarily better. Thanks to Bitcoin's slow speed, though, the world will mostly need to use Layer 2 solutions mentioned in Chapter 6.8 Bitcoin Decentralized Fallacy to support enough traffic to handle the worldwide economy. Interestingly, this "hard work" complexity has created a hardware war to create faster, more efficient specialized computers for mining Bitcoin and other cryptos.

Ethereum is a proof-of-work blockchain. They built Ethereum 2.0 on top of Ethereum as a proof-of-stake blockchain. (Chapter 5.2 Types of Altcoins: Stake Coins.) This goes to show that the industry is not cut and dry, and each coin or token can blur the lines between each type of proof of whatever. Some can even flip on their heads and switch systems as they mature and grow.

You earned:
+25 Understanding
+15 Vocabulary

Continue down this path by reading further or go back to Chapter 5 Subchapter Selection

CHAPTER 5.2
TYPES OF ALTCOINS: STAKE COINS

No, not steak coins. Though, a beef Wellington sounds good just about now; reading a book is hard work!

Some altcoins use proof of staking or proof of liquidity to function. If someone is willing to lock up some sort of digital or digitalized value—temporarily or permanently—inside of a proof-of-staking coin/token, that person earns something in return for the value held. Imagine the wonder and danger if you could place your house's ownership into a token, then use the token as collateral to get a loan. You wouldn't need the permission of a bank, which is both empowering, absolutely mind-boggling, and mind-numbingly terrifying! Or imagine that you have one Bitcoin lying about in cold storage which you are planning to hodl for life. Instead of cold storing it, you could stake it into another project and earn interest by lending it out just like a bank, making your assets work for you.

Proof of liquidity can be immensely powerful for some platforms. Imagine trying to create and run a permissionless cryptocurrency exchange, but you don't have enough cryptocurrencies to do it all by yourself. You would need a considerable sum of each crypto your system plans to exchange. Or you could create a new altcoin system which allows others to join you and get some kind of benefit for becoming part of your system. You could pay gas fees or interest to users who stake their cryptos into your system so your platform has enough liquidity for day-to-day trading. To help balance out the system automatically, you could pay more to users who stake under-represented cryptos in your system and pay less to owners who stake over-represented cryptos. Staking is often at the root of some DeFi, which you can read about in Chapter 5.4 DeFi.

DYOR! Do your own research on steak, errr, stake coins before investing.

You earned:
+25 Vocabulary

Continue down this path by reading further or go back to Chapter 5 Subchapter Selection

CHAPTER 5.3
TYPES OF ALTCOINS: NON-FUNGIBLE

Non-fungible means not equally interchangeable. Unique.

An example of real-world NFTs (Non-Fungible Tokens) are collectible baseball or Pokemon cards (just go with the analogy). No two cards will have exactly the same value. Even two seemingly identical cards will have different attributes that contribute to what someone might be willing to pay or trade for a card; its condition, history, etc. Try trading one White Border 1909–11 T206 Honus Wagner for two #311 1952 Topps Mickey Mantle cards. Try trading a 1999 First Edition Shadowless Holographic Charizard #4 for a Pikachu Illustrator. Hint: these are usually not interchangeable, even if you could get your hands on them.

An example of a fungible cryptocurrency is Bitcoin. Generally speaking, one Bitcoin is equal to any other Bitcoin; it doesn't matter which one you own. Therefore, Bitcoin is fungible. (Each Bitcoin has an on-chain history though, so they are not completely fungible). Technically, Bitcoin is a list of balances and transactions. The Bitcoin ledger does not track "Bitcoins"; it tracks what quantity of Bitcoin resides in each address. Then there is a transaction history to show where it came from.

There are NFTs within the crypto world where each token can be as unique as the paintings in a museum or the faces you see smiling at babies. Each token can be a unique or semi-unique tradable, sellable, valuable, and collectable digital asset. There can be sets of identical tokens within the system, but there don't have to be. For example, there could be one of each of the rarest collectables in a system, but two hundred of some limited-time holiday collectables, and ten million of the common collectables. Alternatively, you could have a system where every single token has unique stats and history. More on this at the bottom of this subchapter.

For example, a game which creates every item with slightly different attributes is creating these items as non-fungible tokens for trading in-game. The difference between in-game items and NFTs is mostly in how they are traded. NFTs can usually be bought, sold, or traded outside of their parent game or system, whereas in-game items must be traded inside the system and within the built-in trading system. It's a fine distinction, and understanding the differences can be helped with a couple fictitious examples:

Imagine a new game company called A Game, Co.

Because this startup is on its A-game (the puns are real here), they choose to include a non-fungible token system within their first game. Clive Owen is one of the first players in the game, and manages to be the first person to tame a dragon. Taming the dragon rewards him "The Breastplate of the Grumpy Old Man." Clive is ecstatic; the item description tells him this item is unique and there will never be another like it in the game. It is a one-time reward for the first player to accomplish this near-impossible feat. Being one-of-a-kind, the item is extremely powerful and gives Clive a clear edge going forward in the game. Word spreads about the prowess of the item, and Clive's popularity grows. Clive chooses not to sell the item to any of the many people who offer him in-game gold or even real-world Bitcoin.

Thanks to the item's benefits, Clive goes on to do well in the game, so when A Game Co. launches its first line of collectable in-game pets, Clive trades some of his in-game gold and buys a very adorable in-game NFT pet cat that his wife nagged the ever-loving snot out of him to purchase. She didn't let him skimp and buy the tabby cat either. She made him buy one of the semi-rare, glow-by-night, undulating-rainbow cats for her.

A year later, A Game Co. comes out with its second game. Clive—having had such success by being one of the first into the other game—hops directly into the new game with vigor. The moment his character enters the game, a pop-up informs him that he can import all of his items from the other game to this one, and the best part is that he gets to keep the breastplate too. The hitch is that he has to retain ownership/control of the non-fungible tokens to keep them in each/both games. "The Breastplate of the Grumpy Old Man" is not as powerful as it had been in the old game, but gives him an edge for his new character, who would have otherwise had no good armor. This boosts Clive's brand-new character slightly, and he quickly succeeds in this new game, all while his wife's adorable NFT cat, Ms. Murder Mittens, follows him around.

When he gets a new, better breastplate, he has to decide if he wants to sell off his one-of-a-kind breastplate for in-game money, real-world money, or to keep it for memory's sake. Also, it's still the best breastplate his character from the first game has, and he doesn't want to give it up, even though he isn't playing that old game anymore. Clive doesn't want to lose his favourite item in both games if he sells the token. He doesn't have a choice about selling the cat, though. His wife had explained to him, gently but seriously, that Ms. Murder Mittens is HER pet cat, but that she'd let him play with it in his games.

In this example, Clive is a participant in a non-fungible token system. It gives him another layer of interest in the game he is playing. It can also create brand loyalty that Clive may carry on into future games by A Game Co., and he could even pass these tokens he has earned down to his children. If A Game Co. allows it, Clive could transfer his NFTs directly into his compatible cryptocurrency wallet and take custody of these tokens, removing them from the A Game Co.'s system. Then Clive could sell or trade them as he sees fit without the permission or involvement of the company. This is what separates NFTs from existing in-game items. It seems like a subtle difference between the old way of "owning" in-game items, but it allows new ways to custody, trade, sell, bequeath, and manage these items in ways that have not even been thought of yet.

As far as A Game Co. is concerned, they love the NFT system. It has brought in additional customers whose only goal is to earn items they can sell for real-world money. A Game Co. can even charge a gas fee for every transfer that happens in their game if they so choose. On the other hand, parents of players may be a bit cranky when they find out their nine-year-old just sold a semi-rare, glow-by-night, undulating-rainbow cat for $500 online to some guy named Clive. They may be doubly miffed when they discover their kid bought $400 of candy and $100 of soda on a whim. (Parents. Will they ever keep up with all this new-fangled internet thingy stuff? And what the heck is an NFT? And where did all this candy come from?!)

Another use for non-fungible tokens is as a way to collect donations or grow a fanbase community. For example, a celebrity or internet-famous video-producing personality can create a new flag or pin piece of NFT artwork each month which only their most loyal followers would buy. The followers can brag about how many flags they own in their profiles while the celebrity gets paid. Some social media platforms already allow users to choose one or more non-fungible tokens to display next to their username. This can help create a sense of community for those who like to spruce up or customize their internet presence. The owner of the NFT system makes money selling these tokens to be used in their system, and the users get a new way of interacting with others on whatever platform they are using. Utilitarians will think these people are nuts, but social butterflies buy these kinds of NFTs like candy. (Utilitarians, though, might consider investing in some early limited-time NFTs to sell later, once the celebrity is more famous.)

Non-fungible tokens are some of the most flexible digital assets out there. Human imagination is the limit.

To muddy the topic a bit, technically, each Bitcoin is not precisely equal to another. Every Bitcoin has a history, and its history could potentially change its perceived value. This means that Bitcoin is mostly fungible. For example, you might not want to own Bitcoin that has been through the Bitcoin wallet of a known drug cartel or terrorist organization. This is also why some people avoid using Bitcoin tumblers—companies that mix your Bitcoin in with others' and randomly hand out Bitcoin from the mixed stockpile to obfuscate where the coins have been—especially since if you send one Bitcoin to them and get one Bitcoin out, you might not be fooling the chainalytics companies. Also, many of these tumblers are straight-up scams that will keep your Bitcoin. For the sake of this book, though, we'll call Bitcoin fungible. It's *mostly* fungible.

You earned:
+100 Bonus Points: Guildorian Coin

Continue down this path by reading further or go back to Chapter 5 Subchapter Selection

CHAPTER 5.4
DEFI

Decentralized finance, or DeFi, is the fairyland of magic and mystery of the crypto world. A decentralized exchange platform is often referred to as a DEX. There are innovative and experimental things happening there which seem like magic to even some of the most consummate numberphiles. In DeFi land, there are also trolls, villains, thieves, and rogues. There are pitfalls, trapdoors, and great treasures at the end of many pathways, or so the legends say.

Seriously though, for many, DeFi at its core is an attempt to replace the function of the banking system with fully or partly decentralized protocols and smart contracts.

DeFi is a lot like the earliest days of the internet. A lot of money is being made, a lot of money is being lost, and every other politician wants nothing more than to ban the entire thing (while secretly investing in their favourites). Imagine a world where not only your money is decentralized (Bitcoin) but your banking can also be decentralized. SushiSwap, Uniswap, and 1inch are just three examples of partially or fully decentralized cryptocurrency exchanges. Bitcoin's primary role in this DeFi world is as a decentralized store of wealth and value. DeFi attempts to add in other traditional banking features such as loans, earning of interest, exchanging of currency pairs, and the stuff you usually have to beg a bank to let you do. DeFi wants no borders, no permissions, no government, corporate, or corruption. DeFi wants a truly free market. Bitcoin and DeFi can also reduce the huge fees associated with traditional finance; this is why it could be so powerful, and why so many in power want to stop it or parts of it at any cost.

To create a DeFi system, a company/person/organization will usually create a platform and a protocol which often has one or more tokens or cryptocurrencies at its core. It tends to rely heavily on smart contracts. Some DeFi are built on top of other cryptos like

Ethereum, Cardano, Polkadot, and many others. Some DeFi are built on top of other DeFi which are built on other platforms which are built on another platform. DeFi is financial Turducken.

DeFi is still in its infancy, and is therefore extremely risky. Just like the 1848–1855 California gold rush, people have made fortunes, people have lost fortunes, and others have lost their lives. Literally, people have been murdered. Search "crypto founders murdered" if it stretches credulity.

If you want to go down the rabbit hole of DeFi learning, start by searching for "MakerDAO wiki," as it is considered by many to be the first DeFi. Also, look up "Uniswap wiki" because they use unicorns instead of fairies! Uniswap is one of the largest, mostly decentralized cryptocurrency exchanges. There're not as much fairies and magic with SushiSwap, but yum! Sushi!

Many or most DeFi are incompatible with or ignore KYC (Know Your Customer). This creates another layer of risk and is one of the reasons governments want to ban and regulate it.

DeFi is in direct competition with the big players, yet DeFi market caps are like ants to a giant. Just like the early internet, expect a rocky road for DeFi. There may be DeFi that flourish and survive, but there will be countless dead DeFi projects on this bloody road to innovation.

Another risk for DeFi is that there is a lot of interconnectivity between DeFi projects, the platforms they are built on, and the stable coins they function with. DeFi projects often have single points of failure which might not be evident until the coin they rely on gets banned, closed down, scammed, hacked, or even just gets sued or investigated by regulators. One day, your DeFi coins could be happily gaining. The next day, they could be worthless, and not at the direct fault of the DeFi token you invested in.

You earned:
+25 Risk
+25 Vocabulary

Continue down this path by reading further or go back to Chapter 5 Subchapter Selection

CHAPTER 5.5
OH YEAH, AND THERE ARE PROOF OF...

...authority, trust, identity, keys, transactions, knowledge, hash rate, capacity, seafood freshness, memes, etc., etc., etc.

There are already so many different types of cryptocurrencies that use all different types of systems to function or secure them. Then, there are variations and combinations galore. Rest assured, there will probably be more types of coins and tokens than you're able to count on a Japanese Soroban abacus.

This complexity and flexibility is part of the reason why it is so important to research all altcoins before purchasing. Altcoins are the Wild West of the crypto world and come with a lot of risks. You cannot compare one coin or token to another directly. You especially can't compare them by only looking at their market caps or the cost of each coin or token of the currency. Altcoins are still in their infancy. Experimentation is rampant in the space, with very little regulation to help protect those who do not do their own research. Even solid research on a coin or token won't guarantee safety when investing. Governments are scrambling to figure out how to mitigate the risks of so many altcoins coming to market so fast. The United Kingdom has already taken steps to ban the sale of cryptocurrency derivatives to help protect the general public from falling for scams and schemes meant to rob them of their money. Or so they say.

Quick examples of use cases:

There may come a day when you can use your crypto wallet to prove your age when buying alcohol without having to show your driver's license. Are you of age in the country you're trying to purchase booze in? Yes, then why do you need to show your driver's license with your name, address, birthday, eye color, etc., to a stranger that might not have your best interests in mind? They only need to know if you are of age in the country you're in at the moment. The spirits store needs a Boolean yes or no, and many of us need more privacy.

Imagine having a proof-of-age token in your digital crypto wallet to share with someone. This token does not tell them anything about you, so you keep your personal information to yourself. The token allows others on that crypto's network to verify who you are when you use your token. The network could then pass on this proof of age to the other party. Good, now you can buy that wine!

A token system could allow proof of authority, providing you access to a resource or information, or enable proof of trust or proof of identity, all without exposing your personal information.

Some existing systems allow you to share a resource you have with the world without exposing that resource directly to the world. You could rent out hard drive space or processing power with proof of capacity. This way, you could prove your resource is available, even when it is not actively in use by this system, allowing a system to be overbuilt. The underutilized users can still get paid for proving they are helping with the project's future growth.

Proof-of-knowledge tokens could be a simple way of keeping a digital résumé of sorts. Every skill you learn, class you complete, or award you win could be held in your crypto wallet to be shared at a moment's notice, with the benefit that you don't have to hand over your personal information, where appropriate. You could use a token in your crypto wallet which proves you have a skill set or license.

Let's try an example where you want to rent a boat and captain it. Your personal information would only be exposed to the vendor if and when there was a problem or incident. The vendor knows that—if you crash the boat—they can get your information from the system, but you know the vendor won't be able to know anything about you if you return the boat in perfect condition. Your information is held safe, and the vendor gets a guarantee for their risk. A smart contract could be set up, optionally with an online arbitration, where you stake an amount of money needed to pay for damages, allowing you to be your own insurance company. This could mean much lower fees for insuring yourself in one-off situations. The opportunity for improving everyday life is endless with blockchain and smart contract technologies.

A real-world example of blockchain and how it can improve life:

https://fishcoin.co/ incentivizes seafood supply chain data capture so the end user can know more about what they are eating.

https://libertarianism.org allows people to get married on the blockchain, an everlasting immutable bond that can be seen by all.

https://www.brooklyn.energy/ lets Brooklyn residents sell their solar power back to the electrical grid.

https://medrec.media.mit.edu/ helps keep medical records secure.

https://dogecoin.com/ a meme/joke turned currency. Every time Elon Musk tweets about it, it sees a small boom. It has sponsored Olympians and NASCAR. It is somehow serious and a meme-based joke all at once. This coin was/is often used as the base currency for trading small-cap altcoins on some exchanges. In January 2021, angry redditors from the subreddit r/wallstreetbets pumped DOGE's price over 1000 percent in one day when they got peeved that traditional markets tried to shut their investing down. Elon Musk promptly tweeted this image, which, for regulatory reasons, probably had nothing at all to do with DOGE crypto pumping 1000 percent in a day because obviously this edition of DOGUE magazine is spelled different:

You earned:
+25 Vocabulary
+100 Understanding
+ 25 Bonus Points: Dogecoin, hehe...

Continue down this path by reading further or go back to Chapter 5 Subchapter Selection

CHAPTER 6
RISKS AND EVERYTHING ELSE

This chapter is not exhaustive! There are risks no one has thought of yet, and this book clearly can't make you aware of every risk. Do your own research. This chapter is designed mostly to get your brain juices flowing and spark some ideas of how some risks might affect you more or less than others. Much of owning Bitcoin comes down to balance. Do you prefer personal safety, asset safety, or a balance of each? What balance of ease of use do you prefer over some level of anonymity?

CHAPTER 6
SUBCHAPTER SELECTION
(Don't tally these points. They're here to help you
choose which subchapter is best for you.)

Chapter 6.1 It Was You, All Along
(Recommended reading for all)
You are your greatest risk. Accept this as fact ASAP, Part 1.
+100 Understanding

Chapter 6.2 Misunderstanding, Kidnapping, Coercion, Torture, Etc.
Other people are the second-greatest risk.
+100 Caution

Chapter 6.3 Bug Out Bag
Be ready for anything, including abandoning your home with your
Bitcoin.
+100 Preparedness

Chapter 6.4 Don't Bet the Farm
Crypto trading is GAMBLING! Be careful!
+100 Gambling

Chapter 6.5 Taxes and Laws
(Recommended reading for all)
Not Texas Laws; Taxes and Laws. It's an important distinction.
+100 Mooching Government

Chapter 6.6 Forever Lost Bitcoin
Don't add to the ever-growing unknown list of Bitcoin lost forever.
-100 Supply vs Demand

Chapter 6.7 Phishing
(Recommended reading for all)

You are your greatest risk. Face this fact ASAP, Part 2.
+100 REKT
+100 Tricked
+100 Duped
-100% Bitcoin

Chapter 6.8 Bitcoin Decentralized Fallacy

Layer 2 exchanges, banks, and services will save Bitcoin.
-100 Decentralized

Chapter 6.9 Excess Paranoia

Don't act paranoid, especially when you think they're watching.
+1042 Paranoia

Chapter 6.10 Electrum Watch-Only Wallet

A cool trick to check the balances of cold-storage Bitcoin.
+100 Awareness
+20 Simplicity

Chapter 6.11 The Three Little Cryptos and the Big Bad Wolf!

The future, maybe, of cryptos.
+100 Future

Oh, how can I help promote this book? All it takes is a like and a comment? That's it? Only a moment of my time would mean that much?! Wow, let's do it! Skip to Chapter 8 Shameless Book Promotion
+100 Awareness
+20 Simplicity

CHAPTER 6.1
IT WAS YOU, ALL ALONG!

The most dangerous risk for Bitcoin is always you and your decisions. When you custody your own Bitcoin wallet, you are your own bank, with all the responsibilities this entails. If you make a mistake and send your Bitcoin to the wrong address, lose your private keys, or even send the wrong type of crypto to a mismatched crypto address (like sending Bitcoin to a Bitcoin Cash address), that Bitcoin could/will be lost forever. There are even some platforms which use different transmission types where you can lose your Bitcoin. Be very careful. You need to thoroughly test any method you plan to use to store your cryptos. Use small amounts of crypto—if possible—to test your method before depositing large amounts. For example, when making Bitcoin wallets in Chapter 4.2 Cold Storage - Hardware Wallet - Professional, you can create fifty bulk addresses and practice transferring a few dollars in and out of a few Bitcoin wallets. Once you are done testing, note that these Bitcoin wallets are now burned and never use them again if their private keys were exposed to the internet, like when using a scraping software. Remember, you are the biggest threat to being your own bank. How you store your Bitcoin holdings will limit or increase this risk.

The second-largest threat to individual Bitcoin wallets is other people. Through social engineering (smooth talking), hacking, insider manipulation, corruption, or bad luck, Bitcoin can be lost or stolen. Whether you keep your Bitcoin in your own cold storage, on exchange, in a service, or in your brain, other people could lose or steal your Bitcoin for you. The Mt. Gox hack alone saw 850,000 Bitcoin stolen. Some of the lost Bitcoin have been recovered through various means, but hacks of that magnitude can wipe out your holdings if you are unlucky. There are many strategies to mitigate the risk, but there isn't one right way. You could consider balancing your portfolio between multiple exchanges and some in cold storage, for example.

There is a non-zero percent chance that the central banks might already own a large enough percent of Bitcoin to control it in the near term, thereby enabling them to manipulate, crash, or cripple the price. There are whales who own enough Bitcoin to dump them on the market, put in a short trade to make a profit as people panic sell, then put in a long position to profit on the way back up as Bitcoin recovers. The larger the market cap of Bitcoin becomes, the more difficult it is for these whales to manipulate the market. Consider that even gold in 2020—at its $9 TRILLION or more market cap—was highly manipulated. Bitcoin, in 2020, had a market cap of a measly $350 million. Those numbers are difficult to fully wrap one's mind around. This means that Bitcoin could be said to be 25,714 TIMES more manipulatable than gold! There is a non-zero percent chance that a whale could drop all of their Bitcoin onto the market at once and crash the price. Whales have actually done this by adding too many zeros to a sell trade by accident. Can you think of anyone who would like to see public trust in Bitcoin crumble as it drops 90 percent from a massive fear sell-off triggered by a whale drop? This could potentially set Bitcoin's price back years or centuries, depending on the market's mood and liquidity post-crash.

It's advised to pay close attention to the governments with some or total control over services and exchanges you choose to use. There is a non-zero percent risk that a government could suddenly change its mind and lock, freeze, or seize all of an exchange's or service's assets. It has happened many times already, and will surely happen again! Using exchanges outside of your country can have some benefits while adding another layer of challenge if something goes wrong. It's a bit of a pain to hop on a boat or plane to demand your money back in person. Consider whether you need to keep your Bitcoin outside of your country of citizenship, or whether it would be more sensible to keep your Bitcoin in your country. In some situations, you could avoid taxes; in others, you could be double taxed. Consider diversifying how you keep your Bitcoin if you are uncertain. Imagine if your country goes to war with the country which holds your Bitcoin or if the country suddenly falls on awful times. How long do you think your Bitcoin will last before it becomes a casualty of war or famine?

Time for a conspiracy theory: There is always the possibility that the central banks could pressure the world's nations into blocking Bitcoin's internet traffic simultaneously. There is no way to end Bitcoin through laws and bans. But—and this is a big but—if the central banks and all major countries of the world simultaneously banned Bitcoin's internet traffic, it could become effectively worthless overnight, regardless of how technically unstoppable Bitcoin might be. There are ways of circumventing firewalls, of course, but we are talking about a worldwide ban and hindrance of Bitcoin. Public trust would plummet, along with the price and usability. The larger Bitcoin becomes, though, the more political pressure there will be from massive institutions heavily invested in Bitcoin. Bitcoin is already fairly large, and has a lot of public and institutional interest and backing.

Time to review some low probability catastrophic events, some of which will present you and your family with more pressing issues than your Bitcoin stack:

If one person/company/organization/government were to have control over 51 percent of the hashpower on the Bitcoin network, they technically could attack the network and create one or more double-spend events. It is assumed, though, that anyone with that kind of hashpower and electricity to run it would make more money and gain political and financial power by not attacking the network and crippling Bitcoin. The cost of such an attack would be astronomical at this point, though a 51-percent attack is always a possibility.

Enough EMP blasts across the world during WW3 (or an alien invasion) could cripple Bitcoin, rendering it useless. But then, you'd be wondering how to get information about what the heck just happened as you walk around your town, gaping at the darkness and the silence of a world with no electricity, cars, functioning machinery, electricity, or electronics.

Future supercomputers or quantum computers could make it possible to crack the Bitcoin safety feature of impossibly large numbers, and someone could drain any Bitcoin wallet they wished. Bitcoin is not anonymous; you can search for "richest Bitcoin wallets." All of the top Bitcoin wallets listed in 2020 held ten thousand Bitcoin minimum, and all of them could be targets for a quantum computer attack. Luckily, Bitcoin has the BIP system which allows it to evolve somewhat, though it would take a fantastic feat to save Bitcoin when that day comes.

The solution would have to come before the problem. On the bright side, these thieves could steal all of the lost Bitcoin and get them back into circulation. This is the biggest takeaway, though. Bitcoin uses a complicated 256-bit encryption method with very long strings. Your email account doesn't come close to as much security with its measly ten-digit password. There is a good chance that the internet would have crashed and the world would be in anarchy as all privacy and accounts become compromised before Bitcoin gets touched. That kind of processing power would enable the users of these hypothetical supercomputers or quantum computers the ability to attack governments and central banks. Why bother with tiny little Bitcoin at that point?

As a last-ditch hope, if all goes horribly wrong, Bitcoin has a trick up its sleeve. Much like a mythical phoenix songbird, Bitcoin can rise from its own ashes. It's called a hard fork. This can literally be a copy/paste of Bitcoin's status a moment before the big bad thing happened, whatever the big bad thing ends up being. Then, before turning this new copy of Bitcoin on, the core protocols can be changed to prevent the problem with new code or new ways of doing things. It's more complicated than what we'll cover in this book, but just know there is still a backup plan if all else fails with Satoshi's original protocols.

This is a fork.

You earned:
+100 Confidence
+25 Risk
+50 Vocabulary

Continue down this path by reading further or go back to Chapter 6 Subchapter Selection

CHAPTER 6.2
MISUNDERSTANDINGS, KIDNAPPING, COERCION, TORTURE, ETC.

This subchapter is a bit darker. There is no 100 percent foolproof way to store your Bitcoin.

Be careful how you distribute your Bitcoin recovery backups. If you give your actual Bitcoin wallet private key or recovery seed phrase to Aunty Karen, and she passes away, someone could crack open her safe and get a very nice surprise when they discover "her" Bitcoin stash. They might not realize—or care—that the Bitcoin belongs to you. And you might be so distraught at the loss of your favourite aunty that you might forget to panic and move all your Bitcoin to a new, secure, temporary Bitcoin wallet. You could consider putting your Bitcoin in a sealed envelope with clear instructions to return it to you, but don't trust that to work. Consider multi-sig in Chapter 4.9 Multi-Signature. This would make Aunty Karen's share of your backup less vulnerable.

There is no foolproof way to keep your Bitcoin. Depending on the amounts you plan to own, how many people think you have large amounts of it (even if you don't actually own any), and the ways you choose to custody your cryptocurrencies, you'll need to consider the risks of kidnapping, coercion, torture, blackmail, and all of the other ways you might be forced to expose your private keys. Like real gold, there is merit in keeping considerable amounts of Bitcoin out of easy reach. If someone thinks you have a large amount of Bitcoin and that you keep it at home, they could try to force you to give them your keys. Again, consider multi-sig in Chapter 4.9 Multi-Signature.

On the other hand, keeping all of your cold storage in some "safe" bank vault also has risks. If there is genuine civil unrest, corruption, etc., private keys in cold storage at your local bank's vault may become unavailable to you if the bank or vault is raided, destroyed, or the bank is closed during the crisis. There is no 100 percent foolproof way to own Bitcoin.

If you own enough Bitcoin to put yourself and your family at risk of an attack, this book is not the place to get your information. You should seriously consider professional advice. There are large-scale custody companies that specialize in risky amounts of asset management, including Bitcoin and other cryptocurrencies. Contact these companies for a custom custodial solution. Ledger is one example. Look for their business solutions on their website. But, did you notice there is no 100 percent foolproof way to own Bitcoin?

You earned:

+125 Risk

+ 25 Bonus Points: Not 100% Foolproof

Continue down this path by reading further or go back to Chapter 6 Subchapter Selection

CHAPTER 6.3
BUG OUT BAG

Emergency preparedness is a highly relevant part to owning Bitcoin which many forget about. Heck, it's a highly relevant piece of LIFE that many forget about. Emergencies happen. The most common insurance claims are wind and hail (tornados, anyone?), fire and lightning (California or Oregon, anyone?), and water damage (burst water pipe, Hurricane Katrina, or Hurricane Sandy, anyone?).

Look, we're not recommending you become a crazy prepper with a bomb shelter or anything. The reality of life is that bad stuff happens. An excellent first-hand account of this sort of emergency experience was written in blog format by Shane at *The Place with No Name*. He recounts his family's experiences evacuating from New Orleans during Hurricane Katrina. This book's author's spouse highly recommends this humorous and sobering look at what to do to keep one's family safe during an emergency.

But there is hope! Shane says that, at the end of the day, you want to get back home. The more Murphy Law–prevention you do before an emergency, the less anxiety you'll have if your neighborhood gets evacuated and/or you're stuck at work fifteen miles away. A good way to alleviate the anxiety is to create a bug out bag and have a plan. If you don't already have a bug out bag, today might be a good day to start making one.

The premise is simple: What are the documents, identifications, paperwork, passwords, passports, hard drives, etc. you would need to rebuild your life if you lost everything else? Organize all that ahead of time; put it all—or backups—in a fireproof document bag. If you have only sixty seconds to get out before your house is destroyed, you can evacuate your partner, your kids, your pets, grab that one single item, and bug out. Speaking of pets, keep your pet carriers functional and accessible for a quick exit.

Especially if you choose to be your own bank and store your Bitcoin in cold storage, consider keeping an encrypted backup copy of your Bitcoin wallet in your document bag. You don't want a fire, earthquake, civil unrest, alien attack, or any other unfortunate emergency to permanently separate you from your Bitcoin backup, especially if it is your only one. Also, you might be able to use the balance in your Bitcoin wallet to barter for food, especially as the world begins accepting Bitcoin in more places, and mobile phones start accepting Bitcoin payments even when offline.

In addition to your life-rebuilding documents and your Bitcoin stash, you can pack a larger bug out bag with emergency survival supplies. You can use the shopping lists Shane provides on his website. Or consider buying a premade bug-out-bag kit with enough food, water, and first aid supplies for all the individuals in your family (and pets that will accompany you).

If you buy a kit, remove the survival supplies from the obvious, cheap, ugly kit bag and put them in a sturdy tactical backpack or a light travel backpack with an extendable handle and rolling wheels. Pick one that's black or dark blue; you don't want to carry a bright red or orange bag that screams, "Come mug me! My bag has the supplies your family needs to survive because you forgot to prep." You want your bug out bag to look like you packed it in old luggage, in a rush, with a sock hanging out the top to show just how useless of a prepper you are and that your bag is probably full of useless clothing. A rolling backpack, even a heavy one, can be worn on the back for crossing small distances, then rolled when on pavement. The ability to roll the bag allows you to carry a little more initially if you can use paved roads. Most people say not to pack too much; others prefer to pack WAY too much stuff, then drop it on the side of the road as they slowly figure out what items are more or less useful in that situation. You can have more than one bug out bag, like a smaller bag in your vehicle. Find a compromise that works for your family.

Two primary bags can be better than one if you have two people who can carry them. Balance the contents by weight, but consider functionality so each bag can be used somewhat individually. Bring some heavy-duty plastic rubbish bags to put your backpacks in if the weather turns on you, or if you need to float your bags across water. You'd be amazed how hard it is to get a heavy bag across a body of water, but how easy it is to drag a floating rubbish bag behind you on a rope.

Emergencies happen. Hopefully they never happen to you. If they do, good luck, be prepared, stay safe, and don't forget your Bitcoin.

You earned:
+150 Difficulty - Because it's really easy not to be prepared.
+50 Bonus Points: I'm not a crazy prepper, but I do have an emergency stash.
+50 Bonus Points: I read Shane's blog.
+50 Bonus Points: I just ordered my bug-out-bag basics off Amazon.

Continue down this path by reading further or go back to Chapter 6 Subchapter Selection

CHAPTER 6.4
DON'T BET THE FARM

This book is not meant to be financial advice but, this book strongly suggests something (that happens to not be financial advice).

Don't bet the farm.

There are many people and organizations out there that would love to get you all excited or chuffed about Bitcoin going up or Bitcoin going down. FOMO—Fear of Missing Out—will get you in a heap of trouble. FUD—Fear, Uncertainty, and Doubt—is equally dangerous to your finances.

If you choose to dabble in Bitcoin trading, you are GAMBLING.

You are gambling against some of the smartest and most experienced traders in the world. They would love the chance to relieve you of your Bitcoin. Don't ever think it's not gambling. No matter how skilled you are, trades can always go bad, or catastrophically bad.

For example, if the price drops faster than your stop loss can trade, you could end up much more upside down than expected, FAST. There are ways of limiting risk, but they only limit risk. They are not a 100 percent foolproof guarantee against risk. Exchanges go down, regulators freeze trading, or your trade may simply fail. There are so many outlier risks that people forget about when they punt and go "all in." Bitcoin lost 50 percent of its value in twenty-seven hours during the black swan event "2020 Corona Dump."

"When you risk more than you can afford to lose, it's almost impossible to be calm and cool-headed enough when things get crazy. And the crypto market is one wild ride." —Friend of the Author.

You are competing against very efficient, automated trading bots and artificial intelligence algorithms which will happily take your Bitcoin. Exchanges that have built-in API (usually found in the settings on their app or website) may have users using automated trading bots that lurk in the transactions, potentially thousands of them at any given moment.

It's not that you can't make money. It's that you need to be aware of your competition. Some exchanges will include small print in their user agreements to skim your transactions for their profit, stealing a couple bucks or Satoshis here and there without you noticing, making your trades a little worse. How were you supposed to know the amount of Bitcoin you bought was supposed to be $25,042 but the exchange showed you it had cost $25,052? They swiped $10 extra in the transaction, and that's not fees; that's just them skimming. Your transactions are mixed up in a blaze of numbers flying across the screen. Verifying that the exchange did or didn't scalp you for a couple bucks is near impossible, especially for the average user.

As they say about the stock market, "past performance is not a guarantee of future returns." Not saying to not trade. If that's what you want to do, great. Do it with money you can afford to lose. Just don't bet the farm.

You earned:
+25 Risk
+25 Understanding

Continue down this path by reading further or go back to Chapter 6 Subchapter Selection

CHAPTER 6.5
TAXES AND LAWS

This book has no tax advice and is not tax advice. The book will hint and nudge and mention that you need to get professional tax advice. If you buy, sell, or profit from Bitcoin and cryptocurrencies, you will likely be subject to taxes. Not only the taxes of your own government, but likely, the taxes of the government where the exchange or service you use resides, potentially resulting in double taxation. Many countries have laws in place, are writing laws, and will write laws so they can get a piece of your Bitcoin wallet. They want your Satoshis, and they want them bad. Don't assume for a second that you are entitled to some form of protection from governments wanting their share because you know:

"Your keys, your Bitcoin. Not your keys, not your Bitcoin"
—Andreas Antonopoulos

Bitcoin does not make you exempt from the real world, and many professional tax advisors would likely recommend following your local tax laws and the laws that govern the taxation of the exchanges and services you use. Tax avoidance is a 100 percent legal (in some countries), but tax evasion will get you thrown in jail (in some countries). There is a fine line between the two; a professional can help. Better to be honest and pay what you owe than to try to hide your gains and get caught, fined, and jailed. Bitcoin is very traceable. Even if you manage to hide your Bitcoin purchase for years by obfuscating it with an OTC purchase, when you go to sell/trade/use it years from now, the government will likely find out and want their piece you owe, with interest.

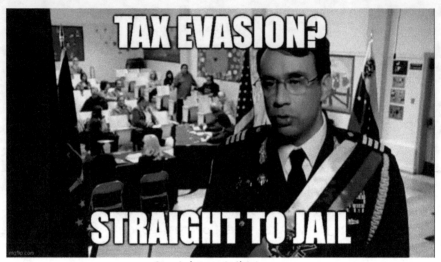

Straight to Jail Meme

You earned:
+50 Confidence

Continue down this path by reading further or go back to Chapter 6
Subchapter Selection

CHAPTER 6.6
FOREVER LOST BITCOIN

There are an unknown number of Bitcoin which have been lost forever. No one knows how many have been lost, though many have tried to guess. All that is known is what shows in the on-chain blockchain data. Within the ledger is all of the data needed to calculate the number of addresses which have not withdrawn any Bitcoin in whatever time frame you are curious about. Or look it up online. Someone else has already done the hard work. Check https://studio.glassnode.com/ for this sort of information and many other interesting charts if that's your thing, you nerd.

There are fascinating charts showing what percentage of Bitcoin has not moved within the last month, year, years, etc. In these charts, you can get a feeling for how many addresses are stacking Bitcoin to hodl for the long term, but you can also try to guess how much Bitcoin has not moved because it was lost. The number of Bitcoin which has been permanently lost will grow, potentially making Bitcoin's value increase. Supply vs demand.

There is a story of a man who lost the private keys to his Bitcoin wallet in the rubbish. There are supposedly around 7500 Bitcoin entombed in the Newport, South Wales landfill on a discarded laptop hard drive. The previous owner has made multiple requests—and even offered large payments—for the right to dig in the municipality's rubbish to find this precious treasure. Under the toxic and corrosive conditions deep within the landfill, successful recovery is unlikely. These lost Bitcoin are a tiny part of a larger pot of forever-lost Bitcoin.

The more Bitcoin that are lost forever, the scarcer Bitcoin gets. Supply vs demand can only get better for Bitcoin over time.

You earned:
+100 Impatience (for lower supply!)

Continue down this path by reading further or go back to Chapter 6 Subchapter Selection

CHAPTER 6.7
PHISHING

Phishing is a real danger. Phishing is social hacking where someone will try to convince you—through some method of communication—to click on a link, download something malicious, expose a password, or do other activities that will expose your accounts and Bitcoin to loss or theft. A great example of this was a hardware wallet manufacturer which had its database of customer information stolen. This database did not directly expose the Bitcoin wallets; still, this hack allowed the attackers to begin an email campaign to try and trick people into downloading corrupted software or hand over access to their recovery seeds and Bitcoin wallet. Successful phishing attacks rely on our trust in others, our trust in technology, our trust in things that seem familiar, and our laziness. Attackers and hackers employ many tricks to get us to compromise ourselves.

A phishing attacker can create a fake website which looks exactly like your bank's website. There may be a slight difference in the web link they hope you won't notice, but they can hide that too. Then, when you try to log in using the fake website, your login information is compromised, your accounts are quickly drained, and you are about to have a very bad day.

It is mostly never advisable to click links from emails or texts, even if they come from trusted sources. The actual link can be hidden behind the text of the link. Click this link for an example: http://www.google.com. If the link works as designed, it won't take you to Google! It will take you to a YouTube video where you can learn about phishing in more detail. (It is possible that it takes you to Google instead if the software you are using to read this book has phishing protection).

One way to defeat some phishing attacks is to go to your web browser and type in the website for your bank, service, or exchange manually, or use bookmarks in your browser that you created and trust. Also, the use of a trusted password management program can help. The password management programs aren't usually fooled by maliciously misspelled web addresses. Be careful, stay paranoid, stay safe.

Even a pirated version of this book could be compromised to alter the links to fool you. If you stole this book, consider buying a real copy to prevent being phished when you click any links. Of course, if the pirates are smart, they will remove or alter this paragraph before compromising all the links, so you'll never know. If they are dumb and left this paragraph unaltered...well, you've been warned.

You earned:
+50 Understanding
+10 Risk

Continue down this path by reading further or go back to Chapter 6 Subchapter Selection

CHAPTER 6.8
BITCOIN DECENTRALIZED FALLACY

(Read the titles of these sections
in your best *Street Fighter* announcer voice).

Layer 1, FIGHT!

Owning your Bitcoin and keeping them in your own custody where you have the actual private keys or seed phrase, is participating in Layer 1. If you assume that Bitcoin is what it seems and that it is not secretly controlled by an evil magician, benevolent but strange alien, or the central banks, you can say that Bitcoin is mostly decentralized. Not one person, group, entity, government, or '80s rock band owns or controls Bitcoin. Not even U2 (the band).

The protocols—code and rules that make Bitcoin work—are open source and have been scrutinized by some of the world's smartest people. At face value, it looks as though Bitcoin will grow or die organically without a central point of leadership or control, only affected by free-market public opinion, investors, and existing and emerging technologies. That is the simple-seeming truth of the Bitcoin protocol. This core code, ledger, and blockchain are called Layer 1.

Layer 2, FIGHT!

Every exchange, service, or bank which allows transactions of Bitcoin is Layer 2. If you buy Bitcoin on any of these, the everyday transactions you make do not get registered on-chain. You also don't own any Bitcoin, not really.

Layer 2 will save Layer 1 Bitcoin—the core on-chain Bitcoin transaction ledger. Bitcoin Layer 1 is not suitable for everyday use. It is extraordinarily slow. This is why Layer 2—banks, services, and exchanges—are required to save Bitcoin.

Bitcoin averages a max speed of 4.6 transactions per second! Many large credit card companies each process well over a thousand transactions in that same second. Bitcoin speed is not significantly increased by having more miners. In simple terms, the Bitcoin protocol is designed to keep the network speed around the same at all times. As more miners join, the difficulty level goes up, slowing it down for the miners, but the overall speed remains the same. As miners leave, the difficulty automatically adjusts to be easier. Therefore, Bitcoin—as it is now—can never be a world transaction currency. This does leave a very important role for Bitcoin: to be one of the world's reserve currencies. Being a reserve of value does not require much speed, especially with Layer 2 to assist. Layer 2 is able to complete an effectively unlimited number of transactions per minute.

Look at Robinhood, PayPal, or any of your favourite exchanges. If you make a transaction on an exchange or service like these, there is little to no chance that your Bitcoin trade will show on-chain. The exchange or service actually owns all of the Bitcoin they custody, and they allow you to pretend you own some of it by having a balance with them. You don't own Bitcoin with these companies; you own a balance. When you make a transaction, they can transfer your balance of the Bitcoin (which the exchange owns/controls) from you to their other user within their own software. As with real gold, huge transactions can be completed without the need to transfer actual physical gold—even between companies and between continents—until two entities decide that the imbalance is too significant. Then they will request a physical delivery or settle in other means. This happens behind the scenes in large corporate transactions daily.

Layer 2, Simple Fun Version:

Samantha owns a hundred marbles. You come to her and give her your money, and she tells you your marble balance is now ten marbles. You don't own any marbles; you have a balance. Then, when you want to give Tarrence one marble in trade for his candy bar, you tell Samantha about it. Now you have a balance of nine marbles and Tarrence has a balance of one marble, all while Samantha owns all the marbles and also has your money.

This is modern banking. All of these transactions happened without anyone else in the marble industry needing to know about it because Samantha owned all of the marbles the entire time. Worst case scenario, if enough of Samantha's marble customers do marble transactions with other marble bankers and Samantha now owes a bunch of marbles to another bank, then the other marble banker may come along and ask for marbles from Samantha to be delivered to them to simplify who owes who what on the banking level.

In summary, Layer 2 will save Bitcoin for general public use. Bitcoin is sluggish and can only handle so much on-chain traffic per minute, but PayPal and the existing exchange systems can handle transactions quietly in the background, off-chain, where they can happily charge you the gas fees and keep these fees for themselves.

Layer 2 will ruin Bitcoin for the maximalists who will watch in horror as more and more Bitcoin slowly sinks into the deep pockets of big money trading. Why do you think exchanges give you huge bonuses to TRANSFER Bitcoin IN, but give small bonuses for depositing money to buy Bitcoin from them?

You earned:
+50 Confidence
+50 Difficulty

Continue down this path by reading further or go back to Chapter 6 Subchapter Selection

CHAPTER 6.9
EXCESS PARANOIA

Don't hide your Bitcoin secrets so well that your beneficiaries can never recover them should you become unavailable, incapacitated, or *permanently unavailable*.

If you trust the people you want to receive your Bitcoin when you have no use for it anymore, consider confiding in and training others on how to get to your super-secret, encrypted, hidden stash. Include instructions for all of your Bitcoin hardware wallets, paper wallets, exchanges, services, banks, etc. It might also be a good idea to give these trusted individuals the login credentials and instructions for every place you keep valuables.

One of the worst things about the passing of a loved one is having to argue with one bank after another, submitting ridiculous documents while you are in mourning. Having a list of all banks, services, exchanges, physical storage units, secret hiding places, and such can alleviate much of the stress of trying to unravel someone's life to see if you've missed anything they might have wanted you to have. Probably also leave instructions for how to delete your browser history...you know...'cause reasons. Probably a good idea to keep a copy of all this information in your sealed will and/or in your bug out bags from Chapter 6.3 Bug Out Bags.

Overcomplication might also cause your heirs problems. It is very easy to think that the plan you come up with today will make sense to you forever. You probably won't remember in a week, and the more complicated it is, the more likely you are to forget what you did. Make sure to take notes on how to get your Bitcoin, and keep the notes in a safe place, in case you might ever sustain a head injury, get amnesia, get old, or just plain forget (probably in a week). Don't make your brain the only place you keep access to large amounts of Bitcoin wealth unless you absolutely have to. Write it down, take notes, keep these safe, and make sure someone you love knows how to use these notes to recover your Bitcoin.

The more complicated you make the process of encrypting, hiding, and protecting your Bitcoin, the more chances there are for errors, damage, loss, theft, and total failure. Trusting a method which requires a particular web page or company or person can create a single point of failure that is unrecoverable. The nice thing about BIP38 encryption and BIP39 seed phrases is that they are agreed-upon methods by the community which remove any company or device from the steps required for recovery. Using the existing safety features of Bitcoin will likely be best for most. See Chapter 2.5 Encryption and BIP.

There are thieves and criminals in the world who do not understand Bitcoin. Bitcoin ATM machines are often broken into when criminals see a lightly armored ATM and assume they can bust it open to grab some Bitcoin and run. This lack of understanding also holds true for your hodled Bitcoin. Before going bonkers and implementing the most foolproof Bitcoin multi-sig, multicontinental scheme you can think of, consider this: what is more important, your Bitcoin or your life? On the off-chance that someone invades your home or does some other horrible thing to demand your Bitcoin, any level of overcomplication could end badly. Take this into consideration before you decide if you prefer robust security or simplified access. Sorry to give you the burden of knowledge, but this chapter is called Excess Paranoia for a reason.

Don't make it too hard on yourself. Remember, you are probably the number one risk of failure. Other people are the second-largest risk. There is always someone out there who wants your Bitcoin. But you also want your Bitcoin, so don't go overboard with paranoia and complications.

You earned:
+100 Bonus Points: Trust No One.

Continue down this path by reading further or go back to Chapter 6 Subchapter Selection

CHAPTER 6.10
ELECTRUM WATCH-ONLY WALLET

As mentioned in Chapter 4.5 Cold Storage - Software Wallet, Electrum is a computer software for creating, monitoring, and using Bitcoin wallets which can be managed on a computer. Even if you are not going to use Electrum for this, you can use it to periodically check the balances of a list of any public addresses you find interesting. This could be a list of the hundred largest Bitcoin wallets or it could be a bulk list of public addresses you created in Chapter 4.6 Cold Storage - Paper Wallet - Digital Version. With Electrum, you can easily check your balances for whatever reason.

Download and install Electrum from https://electrum.org. Make sure you use .org and not .com. Use whatever method they suggest to make sure you have a legitimate download which has not been compromised. Install it.

1. When creating a new Electrum wallet, give it a name. It could be something like "Watch-Only Wallets" as an example.
2. Choose "Import Bitcoin addresses or private keys."
3. Enter the PUBLIC addresses you want to check into the box. Each line should be a different address. Do not put any private keys into this form for a watch-only wallet.
4. Create a password. Being a view-only wallet, the password may not need to be very secure.
5. Optionally, once it loads, you can click on the "Addresses" tab at the top of the software, then you can double click on the "Label" column for each address you want to provide a label to.

You earned:
+25 Nerdiness

Continue down this path by reading further or go back to Chapter 6 Subchapter Selection

CHAPTER 6.11
THE THREE LITTLE CRYPTOS
AND THE BIG BAD WOLF!

Imagine for a moment a future in which the world governments are building and implementing a new CBDC (Central Bank Digital Currency) system. You already live in a somewhat digital world, but you can still get access to cash and use it as you see fit for the most part. A CBDC could end that anonymity and freedom through control, though there would always be a subset of people who refuse to allow all of their worth to be in direct control of their governments. In an (apocalyptic) CDBC world, governments could freeze or reduce your funds without notice simply because of your viewpoints. They could disallow people of a certain poverty level the right to buy cigarettes or alcohol "for their own good." Imagine always wondering if the government will come down on you because you eat too much fast food or like to buy physical gold. Maybe it would be something like taxes which increase the more you spend on junk food per month.

We already live in a world where some people fear a banking collapse or have witnessed one first-hand. You live in a world where people distrust their governments and the central banks. These people tend to buy physical gold or silver as a store of a portion of their wealth if they can afford it. Bitcoin and other cryptos allow someone to do the same thing, but protect it even better. If a thief enters your house and finds your gold, it's gone. If a thief finds your well-protected and backed up crypto stash, who cares. When you get home and find out your crypto wallet is gone, you can call Uncle Bob, go get your backup seed phrase, and quickly transfer your funds to a new wallet. Your government will not have direct control over your funds if they are self-custodied Bitcoin. There could be a near future where a mass majority of people who can afford it rely on various cryptos for hedging and wealth preservation while letting the poor or uneducated use the CDBC system blindly.

This subchapter is titled "The Three Little Cryptos" as a reference to the three little pigs, not three specific cryptos; there is no crystal ball for what is coming. Undoubtedly, Bitcoin will not be the only store of value people use. Bitcoin may be digital gold, but there is also digital silver and digital copper. Will there be a future where Bitcoin is a "precious crypto"? Will there be a secondary precious crypto equivalent to physical silver? Ethereum is already making huge strides to becoming an industrial crypto, equivalent to copper being an industrial metal. Some who call Bitcoin digital gold call Ethereum digital oil.

There is a lot of competition right now as the crypto world matures. Whatever coins and altcoins come out on top, there is a good chance many people will feel safer keeping a portion of their net worth safe. The big bad wolves will show themselves soon enough. What will push people to trust crypto more than their own leadership and banking system? Will it be Central Bank bail-ins? Or the freezing or confiscation of assets of some famous contrarian the public sympathizes with? Will it be a government that decides what you can eat, what vices you are allowed access to, and where you can spend your money? Will it be retail investors finding out that wall street has a different set of rules? Will it be countries trying to break out of sanctions, break out of hyperinflation? Will it be everyone trying to escape the sinking ship that is debt-based fiat? What will it be that pushes the masses into the open arms of the crypto world?

You earned:
+50 Bonus Points: Trust No One

Continue down this path by reading further or go back to Chapter 6 Subchapter Selection

CHAPTER 7
WHO ARE YOU, ADVENTURER?

You made it! It's time to find out who you are.

You earned:
+25 Vocabulary - If you referenced the glossary at least once.
+50 Vocabulary (Additional) - If you referenced the glossary at least twice.
+125 Vocabulary (Additional) - If you feel like you referenced the glossary every chapter.

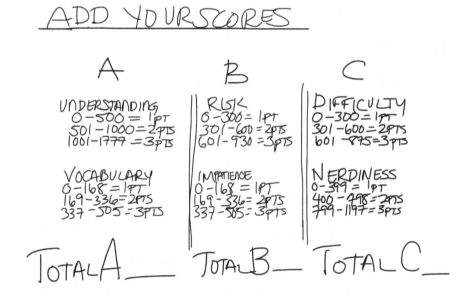

ADD YOUR SCORES

A

UNDERSTANDING
0 - 500 = 1 PT
501 - 1000 = 2 PTS
1001 - 1777 = 3 PTS

VOCABULARY
0 - 168 = 1 PT
169 - 336 = 2 PTS
337 - 505 = 3 PTS

TOTAL A ___

B

RISK
0 - 300 = 1 PT
301 - 600 = 2 PTS
601 - 930 = 3 PTS

IMPATIENCE
0 - 168 = 1 PT
169 - 336 = 2 PTS
337 - 505 = 3 PTS

TOTAL B ___

C

DIFFICULTY
0 - 300 = 1 PT
301 - 600 = 2 PTS
601 - 875 = 3 PTS

NERDINESS
0 - 399 = 1 PT
400 - 798 = 2 PTS
799 - 1197 = 3 PTS

TOTAL C ___

TOTAL A:

If you scored...

- 2–3: You've got the basic road map for your journey, but consider reading more and learning more. You'll never regret having too much information—unless it stops you from getting out there on the road!
- 4: You have a solid grasp of how you want to own your Bitcoin. Get out there and do it!
- 5–6: You're the master. You are now expected to publish the next bestseller on Bitcoin. Great job!!

TOTAL B:

If you scored...

- 2–3: You tend to take more time to analyze information, even if it's not what you're looking for. Open up to learning more and increasing your risk tolerance.
- 4: You are fairly conservative with your risk tolerance, but are willing to take chances. Go out there, find the strategy that works best for you, and implement it!
- 5–6: You are a risk taker while still controlling your risks! Get out there and stack them Satoshis!

TOTAL C:

If you scored...

- 2: Be cautious before you implement any Bitcoin-owning strategies! Read up on the recommended chapters.
- 4: You know enough to be dangerous. DYOR and have a great time!
- 5–6: You are a supernerd. Your nerdiness and willingness to take on hard stuff is the stuff of legends. Just don't get too tied up in the details; get going on your journey to owning Bitcoin!

If you are short on points, make sure you've read all of the Chapter 9 Miscellaneous Interesting Stuff - Rated: Everyone to stock up on some extra points, pad your score a bit.

If you got Adorableness points, you are a fine human being. Keep being awesome! You win life; go eat a healthy snack.

If you actually kept your score throughout the book, you should be proud of yourself! You are one of the few who aces magazine quizzes, excels at internet surveys, and is genuinely introspective. Thank you for engaging with this book!

Bonus points: 15–500: Thanks for playing the game with us! Wanted to do something humorous and fun, so hope these kept it light for you. Thanks for reading!

Lastly, add up the final scores for each of the final score things. If you got between 6–24 points, eat that many crisps or candies and drink a glass of water for your health. If you can't eat crisps and candy, well, then you still win: give yourself a salt-free, sugar-free hug.

CHAPTER 8
SHAMELESS BOOK PROMOTION

There is a non-zero percent chance that it would mean the world to us if you would rate the book and leave a comment reviewing it. Amazon's algorithm likes to see reader engagement, so please consider rating this book on Kindle and leaving a comment if it helped you. Every rating and comment tells the algorithm you were engaged with the material. This engagement boosts whether Amazon chooses to recommend this book to others looking for this same type of information. Consider leaving a review of the book as your comment. You are 100% allowed to copy/paste small amounts of text from this book if you need to use it in your review!

Thanks for taking this journey with us, Adventurers! You now have a mountain of information, an understanding of risk, the burden of knowledge, and the comfort level of convenience. It's time to choose what's right for you, and it's time to make your way through the world of Bitcoin.

Stay paranoid, curious, and DYOR!

<{ Jason Aralia }>

CHAPTER 9
MISCELLANEOUS INTERESTING STUFF

Genesis

The Ireland-based band U2 seems to love being first in new technologies, like including music tracks on new phones. U2 didn't manage to get this gig with Bitcoin, though; instead, this book is talking about Genesis. No, not the Godalming, Surrey, band Genesis. *Genesis* as in the beginning, the very first block in the Bitcoin blockchain.

When Satoshi Nakamoto and accomplices mined the very first block of Bitcoin, they left us a little Easter egg. The image below shows the raw hexadecimal data for the genesis block, and on the right column is the ASCII text translation. Magic and fairies again, creating words from numbers. Hex? ASCII? What this means is that the data from the first block of Bitcoin was intentionally crafted so it would include the message "The Times 03/Jan/2009 Chancellor on brink of second bailout for banks."

The text hidden in the hex data for the genesis block is a reference to a news article from *The Times* newspaper which made the front cover on January 3rd, 2009. This hidden text seems to fit Satoshi Nakamoto's vision of a decentralized banking system by showing the world an example of the existing system's failures. It also provides us with an on-chain, verifiable earliest date in which the first block could have been mined.

```
00000000  01 00 00 00 00 00 00 00  00 00 00 00 00 00 00 00   ................
00000010  00 00 00 00 00 00 00 00  00 00 00 00 00 00 00 00   ................
00000020  00 00 00 00 3B A3 ED FD  7A 7B 12 B2 7A C7 2C 3E   ....;£íýz{.²zÇ,>
00000030  67 76 8F 61 7F C8 1B C3  88 8A 51 32 3A 9F B8 AA   gv.a.È.Ã^ŠQ2:Ÿ¸ª
00000040  4B 1E 5E 4A 29 AB 5F 49  FF FF 00 1D 1D AC 2B 7C   K.^J)«_Iÿÿ...¬+|
00000050  01 01 00 00 00 01 00 00  00 00 00 00 00 00 00 00   ................
00000060  00 00 00 00 00 00 00 00  00 00 00 00 00 00 00 00   ................
00000070  00 00 00 00 00 00 FF FF  FF FF 4D 04 FF FF 00 1D   ......ÿÿÿÿM.ÿÿ..
00000080  01 04 45 54 68 65 20 54  69 6D 65 73 20 30 33 2F   ..EThe Times 03/
00000090  4A 61 6E 2F 32 30 30 39  20 43 68 61 6E 63 65 6C   Jan/2009 Chancel
000000A0  6C 6F 72 20 6F 6E 20 62  72 69 6E 6B 20 6F 66 20   lor on brink of
000000B0  73 65 63 6F 6E 64 20 62  61 69 6C 6F 75 74 20 66   second bailout f
000000C0  6F 72 20 62 61 6E 6B 73  FF FF FF FF 01 00 F2 05   or banksÿÿÿÿ..ò.
000000D0  2A 01 00 00 00 43 41 04  67 8A FD B0 FE 55 48 27   *....CA.gŠ.ý°þUH'
000000E0  19 67 F1 A6 71 30 B7 10  5C D6 A8 28 E0 39 09 A6   .gñ¦q0·.\Ö¨(à9.¦
000000F0  79 62 E0 EA 1F 61 DE B6  49 F6 BC 3F 4C EF 38 C4   ybàê.aÞ¶Iö¼?Lï8Ä
00000100  F3 55 04 E5 1E C1 12 DE  5C 38 4D F7 BA 0B 8D 57   óU.å.Á.Þ\8M÷º..W
00000110  8A 4C 70 2B 6B F1 1D 5F  AC 00 00 00 00            ŠLp+kñ._¬....
```

Rated: EVERYONE

There are a few parts of this book that are recommended as reading for EVERYONE, no matter if you're a total noob or a Bitcoin maximalist. Please consider taking the time to read these sections:

Chapter 2.1 Fundamentals
Chapter 3.3 ETFs
Chapter 3.6 Dollar-Cost Averaging
Chapter 4.1 Cold Storage - Hardware Wallet - Smartphone with TEE Chip
Chapter 4.9 Multi-Signature
Chapter 6.1 It Was You, All Along
Chapter 6.5 Taxes and Laws
Chapter 6.7 Phishing

GLOSSARY OF TERMINOLOGY

This list of Bitcoin-related terminology is defined in a way that works for this book and is not exhaustive, not even complete, and probably not as accurate as it could possibly be. Enjoy!

256-bit	In terms of Bitcoin, 256-bit refers to the kind of encryption used.
altcoin	Cryptocurrencies and tokens other than Bitcoin or Ethereum.
API	Software-to-software data requests and data exchange. API is the social distancing of the software world.
bags or bagholders	*Bags* is an unfancy word for portfolio.
BIP	The Bitcoin Improvement Proposals found at https://github.com/bitcoin/bips are community agreed–upon methodologies that improve Bitcoin by standardizing how certain things are done. Read more in Chapter 2.5 Encryption and BIP.
BIP38 encryption	Simple version: A community agreed–upon way to encrypt Bitcoin wallets with a passphrase.
BIP39-compliant seed phrase	Simple version: A community agreed–upon method to simplify the backup information needed for Bitcoin wallets by using recognizable words.
Bitcoin	Chapter 1.1 Basics.
Bitcoin maximalist	A person who believes Bitcoin will take over as the world reserve currency or equivalent.

Bitcoin Pizza Day	On May 22, 2010, Laszlo Hanyecz paid 10,000 Bitcoin for two pizzas. Often considered to be the birthday of Bitcoin having a cash value.
Bitcoin wallet	Chapter 2.2 Private Keys.
blockchain	See glossary for **ledger**.
brain wallet	An alphanumeric Bitcoin wallet that you can remember. These kinds of wallets are for extreme cases. One way these can be created is outlined in Chapter 4.6 Cold Storage - Paper Wallet - Digital Version.
bulk wallet	A list of more than one Bitcoin wallet. One way these can be created is listed in Chapter 4.6 Cold Storage - Paper Wallet - Digital Version.
CBDC	Central Bank Digital Currency.
chainalytics	The analysis and study of cryptocurrency blockchains to ascertain information about the companies and people who use the networks.
cryptocurrency	Currency that only exists online or in digital format that is based on cryptology.
custody	Ownership or stewardship.
decentralized	Meaning that no single person, government, organization, or evil Bond villain has direct control.
DeFi	/Dee-Fy/ *Decentralized Finance* is the merger of cryptocurrencies and smart contracts to mimic and potentially replace traditional banking.
digital currency	Currency that only exists online or in digital format.
DYOR	Do Your Own Research! Seriously.

ETF	Exchange-traded fund—is a type of investment fund.
exchange	A company or protocol which allows the trading of cryptocurrencies and/or fiat currencies.
exploits	Problems within a software or smart contract which can be exploited by hackers maliciously.
fiat currency	Money, created by a government, without having an intrinsic value.
Flippening, The	1. The hypothetical moment that Ethereum maximalists get to say, "We told you so," and Ethereum becomes the dominant cryptocurrency. 2. Can also refer to Bitcoin surpassing physical gold's various evaluations.
FOMO fomoing in fomoing out	Fear of Missing Out. Generally refers to opportunities to buy Bitcoin because of large moves in trend, but which are not beneficial to the purchaser (like buying at the top of the market, just before a huge correction).
fork or hard fork	The act of copy/pasting an existing cryptocurrency to create a new one.
gas fees	The fees paid to do a transaction in a cryptocurrency.
hardware wallet	A piece of hardware that allows for the management and secure storage of Bitcoin wallet information. It also aids with creating and signing transactions.
hodl or hodling	Hodl and its derivatives are intentional meme misspellings of the word hold.
KYC	Know Your Customer. Many countries use KYC where customers have to provide proof of identity to open an account or transfer money.

Ledger (device)	A hardware wallet made by ledger.com that has closed source proprietary software. Chapter 4.2 Cold Storage - Hardware Wallet - Professional.
ledger	A detailed history of every transaction on a crypto, usually public knowledge.
mining	Using computers and specialized hardware to run the Bitcoin protocol, support the network, and secure the network for a chance to earn Bitcoin rewards.
non-fungible/fungible	Chapter 5.3 Types of Altcoins: Non-Fungible.
open source	Software that is freely available to the public for viewing or editing.
paper wallet	A Bitcoin wallet created so it can be written down or printed out on paper or other mediums. Just because a paper wallet can be printed or written down does not mean it has to be on paper to call it a paper wallet.
permissionless	There is no person, government, organization, or evil villain who can allow or deny you a Bitcoin wallet, though they might try.
Ponzi scheme	A money scheme where each lower layer of participants pays the layer above. They can make a lot of money fast, but are unsustainable. Bottom-level participants at the end lose, and harshly. Google "Bernard Madoff."
private key	Chapter 2.2 Private Keys.
public address	Chapter 2.4 Public Address.
pump and dump	The value of a crypto going up quickly then falling quickly. Sometimes it refers to intentional manipulation or theft.

recovery phrase	See **seed phrase**.
sandbox, sandboxed	An electronic device that has been isolated from the internet and other potential outside risks.
Satoshi Nakamoto	The pseudonym for the inventor of Bitcoin.
Satoshi Satoshis Sats	0.00000001 Bitcoin. There are 100 million Satoshis per Bitcoin.
seed phrase	See **BIP39-compliant seed phrase**.
self-custody	Ownership or stewardship done by oneself.
sign	Bitcoin transactions must be signed using the Bitcoin wallet's private key. Software and hardware wallets can assist with this.
smart contracts	Contracts built on logic that are partly or fully automated by data.
stackin' Sats stacker	Terms some use to describe buying Bitcoin whenever possible to own as many as reasonable.
staking	The act of placing cryptocurrencies into a smart contract to gain something in return. Not to be confused with steaking or barbecuing.
sweeping	The process of using a Bitcoin private key to "sweep" all of the Bitcoin out of it into another address.
to the moon/mooning	A phrase used to describe the Bitcoin price going up very significantly.
token	A unit in a blockchain project which has a use other than for payments. *Coin* and *token* are somewhat interchangeable, and the line between them is often blurred.

Turducken or three-bird roast	A food item where a deboned chicken is stuffed into a deboned duck that is stuffed into a deboned turkey then cooked, creating a layered meat. *Turducken* therefore refers to something that is layers and layers of different things.
vaporware	A derogatory term for digital assets which are not tangible.
whale	A person, government, organization, or evil villain who owns large amounts of Bitcoin. They can manipulate the price somewhat through large transactions.
White paper	A detailed description on a topic.

AFFILIATE LINKS

Many of the external links in this book are affiliate links. The author of this book receives a benefit from readers using these links if they use the services. It is your responsibility to research these companies on your own before using them. There is often a benefit to the reader for signing up for services using these affiliate links, so check if the bonuses are worth it to you before you sign up, but the author would really appreciate it if you signed up using these links for the services you plan to use. Thanks.

https://r.kraken.com/HowToOwnBitcoin
Kraken was the first United States exchange to receive a banking license. It is mostly a trading platform, but can also be used to buy and hodl Bitcoin and cryptocurrencies. They allow withdrawals to cold storage as of the time of this book's first publishing.

https://www.coinbase.com
Coinbase is one of the largest United States Bitcoin exchanges with two versions: https://www.coinbase.com is their simpler design, and it integrates smoothly with https://pro.coinbase.com, which has been designed with trading in mind. (Notice the "pro" in the link for the pro site.) The sites are separate crypto wallets and balances, but you can easily transfer your funds between the two accounts. It seems as though https://pro.coinbase.com charges lower fees and allows more advanced features.

https://www.swanbitcoin.com/HowToOwnBitcoin
Swan Bitcoin lets you set up automatic purchases of Bitcoin at weekly or monthly intervals. This lets you "Dollar-Cost Average," and can be a powerful strategy for buying Bitcoin if you don't want to try and time the market. See chapter Chapter 3.6 Dollar-Cost Averaging. They also allow one-time purchases. Swan Bitcoin does not custody

your Bitcoin, so you'll need to supply them with a public address to send your Bitcoin to, or you can use their partner to custody it for you.

https://exchange.blockchain.com/trade?referrerUsername=HowTo OwnBitcoin

A large crypto exchange. One of the reasons many use this site is the ability to sweep addresses of cold storage and paper wallets. This lets you clear out a wallet you no longer need.

Ledger is a manufacturer of hardware wallets with closed source software. Their Ledger Nano S and Ledger Nano X are popular products. Check Chapter 4.2 Cold Storage - Hardware Wallet - Professional for information on using hardware wallets. It is recommended to get the Ledger Backup Pack Bundle that comes with one Nano S and one Nano X. Each device is an independent hardware wallet. You can keep the bulk of your Bitcoin and other cryptos on one Ledger Nano to keep in your safe or somewhere safe. Then you can use the other Ledger Nano for smaller transactions or carry it with you while exposing less of your Bitcoin to daily risks. Another use for two Ledgers is to load one with a small amount of Bitcoin and put your bulk Bitcoin in the other. Make sure a thief can find the smaller decoy wallet instead of your other. The company also creates business solutions for large-scale cold storage.

Ledger Nano X
https://shop.ledger.com/products/ledger-nano-x?r=36a05bea1a87&tracker=HowToOwnBitcoin

Ledger Nano S
https://shop.ledger.com/products/ledger-nano-s?r=36a05bea1a87&tracker=HowToOwnBitcoin

Ledger Backup Pack (Recommended)
https://shop.ledger.com/products/ledger-backup-pack?r=36a05bea1a87&tracker=HowToOwnBitcoin

Trezor manufactures the most popular open source hardware wallet. Their Trezor One and Trezor Model T are their flagship products. These hardware wallets are supported on many specialized websites which custody one of your multi-sig shares for stronger security. See Chapter 4.9 Multi-signature. Check Chapter 4.2 Cold Storage - Hardware Wallet - Professional for information on using hardware wallets. If you get more than one device, they will have independent wallets on them, in case you need to split your cryptos: one for day-to-day transactions and one for your hodl.

Trezor Model T - Black
https://shop.trezor.io/product/trezor-model-t?offer_id=15&aff_id=6003&source=HowToOwnBitcoin

Trezor One - Black
https://shop.trezor.io/product/trezor-one-black?offer_id=35&aff_id=6003&source=HowToOwnBitcoin

At their site, you'll find the two models in more colors. You'll also find steel seed phrase storage devices that can withstand a beating, fire, minor flood, etc. Take a look:
https://shop.trezor.io/?offer_id=10&aff_id=6003&source=HowToOwnBitcoin

https://unstoppabledomains.com/r/c92afe46a3304ea
Unstoppable Domains allows you to have a simple version of your public addresses for Bitcoin and altcoins. Instead of having 175hXmhiKQdETv5R8fAFdRoKAofbg53ja4 for Bitcoin and 0xe8F6eDF2425482C7945e47b325404e57e27ece7C for Ethereum as addresses, you can have something like HowToOwnBitcoin.crypto as one simple personalized address. Once you buy an Unstoppable Domain token and transfer it into a compatible wallet, like the Coinbase wallet app, you own the link and no one can take it from you directly. But don't go buying a copyrighted brand name and think they won't wreck you in court until you relinquish it to them "voluntarily."

As an example, HowToOwnBitcoin.crypto can accept both Bitcoin and Ethereum donations, and if you need practice sending Satoshis to an Unstoppable Domains address, you could leave a tip if you love the book, hint, hint. You can't put this address into any normal http browser. These special links created at https:// unstoppabledomains.com/r/c92afe46a3304ea are not normal links; to use them, they do require special plug-ins on apps. If they become more commonplace, integration will also become more common. Your public addresses will be searchable through sites like https://viewblock.io/unstoppable so people will be able to see your activity and balances. Unstoppable Domains affords some, but not total anonymity. Having an Unstoppable domain also lets you have a permanent, decentralized website that is permissionless and immutable.

https://3commas.io/?c=HowToOwnBitcoin

3Commas is a trading bot software that runs in the cloud. You can provide them with API access to your exchange and let the bot do automatic trading for you. Though that might sound amazing, the real reason many use 3Commas is their SmartTrade feature. This can allow you to add functionality to your trading which your exchange does not support natively. For example, you could use the SmartTrade feature manually to buy an altcoin you have interest in. If you set the SmartTrade up correctly, the 3Commas bot can track your trade and take advantage of features like multiple take profits, trailing take profits, stop loss timeouts, trailing stop losses, and trailing buy. For the most part, 3Commas is a tool for use by experienced traders.

https://use.foldapp.com/r/M3FWVLRT

Fold App is a credit card company that integrates cryptos!

https://www.tradingview.com/gopro/?share_your_love=HowToOwnBitcoin

This site lets you explore the price charts for so many different cryptos, commodities, fiats, stocks, etc. You can use the service for free, and even set up alarms for price changes to be sent to your phone if you use their app, or sent to email or text messages.

Typing "BTCUSD" in the Symbol Search will give you a list of many exchanges that support Bitcoin. It can be advantageous to choose the exchange you will be trading on, especially for trading in very small time frames. But there are also advantages to choosing an exchange with large trading volume, as the chart may look cleaner if you are trading on longer time frames.

Typing "ETHBTC" would let you see how Ethereum is doing in comparison to Bitcoin.

Try typing "CRYPTOCAP:BTC.D" into the Symbol Search. This will give you a chart of the Bitcoin Market Cap Dominance against a basket of other cryptos. You can use this as an indicator to see if Bitcoin is growing faster than the combined top cryptos, or if your money might be better invested in altcoins sometimes.

Try typing "TVC:DXY" into the Symbol Search. This will give you the US dollar compared against a set of foreign currencies as an indication of the strength of the US dollar.

"CME:BTC1!" Will give you Bitcoin Futures on the CME. This is one way to check for "CME gaps" that some Bitcoin traders believe in.

"OTC:GBTC" Will give you the price chart of the Grayscale Bitcoin ETF that can be purchased inside many self-managed retirement funds.

ABOUT THE AUTHOR, ENGAGEMENT, AND DONATIONS

The author is a really nice guy, some say. Born at a relatively young age, he quickly realized his passion for gazelle taming, but has yet to be successful. In his spare time, which was limited, he enjoyed writing this book while nursing his gazelle injuries. Don't bother coming for the author's Bitcoin; he's poor. Why else write a book? Also, his tiny hodl of Bitcoin is safe. If you didn't notice, the author is paranoid and good at making their Bitcoin very difficult to get to, even for themselves.

If you don't mind helping, Amazon's algorithm likes to see reader engagement, so please consider rating this book on Kindle and leaving a comment or review. Such a simple thing would mean the world for this book's exposure. Thank you in advance!

The author really doesn't expect or need donations as much as ratings and comments wherever you purchased this book. But if you enjoyed this book and feel the need to donate Bitcoin to the author, you can use this address 12LMgBAHJDvwK6p6iBsBeFzVK2VStU97pk. You can also use it if you want to see just how transparent Bitcoin can be, since you can search the web for sites that will let you see the balance and all of the transactions of an address. Paste in this address to see if the author has been gifted any Satoshis, drop a tip and you'll be written into the ledger for all time as a kind and giving individual. The QR code below can be scanned into apps for either donating or for snooping. Alternatively, if you need practice sending Bitcoin or Ethereum to an UnstoppableDomains address, you can use the address HowToOwnBitcoin.crypto on compatible websites, browser plug-ins, and apps. See affiliate links for more about UnstoppableDomains.

Rate this book, leave a comment, leave a review.
It really does mean the world to me. Thanks.

DYOR! Jason, Out.

www.ingramcontent.com/pod-product-compliance
Lightning Source LLC
La Vergne TN
LVHW051340050326
832903LV00031B/3647